Naughty But Nice
Cross Stitch

Claire Crompton

D&C
David and Charles

www.mycraftivity.com

A DAVID & CHARLES BOOK

Copyright © David & Charles Limited 2009

David & Charles is an F+W Media Inc. company
4700 East Galbraith Road
Cincinnati, OH 45236

First published in the UK and US in 2009

Text and designs copyright © Claire Crompton 2009
Layout and photography copyright © David & Charles 2009

ISBN-13: 978-0-7153-2950-4 hardback
ISBN-10: 0-7153-2950-2 hardback
ISBN-13: 978-0-7153-2951-1 paperback
ISBN-10: 0-7153-2951-0 paperback

Printed in China by Shenzhen Donnelley Printing Co. Ltd.
for David & Charles
Brunel House   Newton Abbot   Devon

Senior Commissioning Editor: Cheryl Brown
Editor: Bethany Dymond
Assistant Editor: Kate Nicholson
Project Editor and Chart Preparation: Lin Clements
Designers: Eleanor Stafford and Mia Farrant
Photographers: Kim Sayer and Karl Adamson
Production Controller: Ros Napper

Visit our website at www.davidandcharles.co.uk

David & Charles books are available from all good bookshops; alternatively
you can contact our Orderline on 0870 9908222 or write to us at
FREEPOST EX2 110, D&C Direct, Newton Abbot, TQ12 4ZZ (no stamp
required UK only); US customers call 800-289-0963 and Canadian
customers call 800-840-5220.

Contents

Housework
can't kill you—
but why take
the chance?

I'm a DOMESTIC ANGEL

if you ever see me cook
it'll be a MIRACLE

Introduction

This collection of cross stitch sayings with attitude is for the modern woman who has had her fill of sweet sentiments and who is looking for expressions that are sassy and sharp. With all the demands on her time – work, family, housework – there's barely room for the important things in life, such as chocolate, cupcakes, wine and shoe shopping. When men, children and in-laws have driven her to distraction, she'll discover how she can get rid of her frustration in a mature, calm way, by stitching designs that are ever so naughty but nice (well, almost).

There are nine chapters, each one with its own design theme.

* **Ageing Disgracefully** oozes1950s glamour, helping you to defy the effects of each passing year and encouraging you to have fun, whatever your age.
* **Work Woes** offers cheeky designs to help you get through the office politics and paperwork.
* **Born to Shop** celebrates a favourite pastime for many of us and proves that a girl can never have enough shoes, handbags or credit cards.
* **Domestic Bliss** has yellow gingham and daisies, to cheer you up as you do the dusting.
* **Christmas Chaos** features some harassed fairies fed up, perhaps like you, with having to do all the work to make the event a success.
* **Food For Thought** brings you tempting cupcakes, so you can have your cake even if the diet says not to eat it.
* **Men are from Mars...** pokes fun at romance with sentiments that have a sting in the tail.
* **Family Fun**, with its home-spun designs, shows you love your family really, despite the mess, the tantrums and the relatives.
* **Saving the Planet** has organic flower power that will make taking out the recycling seem positively glamorous.

Detailed making up instructions are given in each chapter so you can recreate the projects shown or use the designs in other ways. The stitching techniques needed are on pages 98–100.

These designs spell out that life is not to be taken too seriously; there's room for humour in our stressed world. So kick off your shoes, open a box of chocolates, ignore the housework and settle down to some stitching therapy.

Say no to dreary housework, at least for a little while, as you stitch these fun designs – perfect to give as gifts to like-minded friends.

Ageing Disgracefully

Why do we have to be sensible as we get older? It's nice to be nice but much more fun being naughty, so ignore the advice for growing old gracefully and become an embarrassment to your children.

The six designs in this chapter feature fabulously elegant women who prove the adage that you're only as old as you feel. Keep yourself looking gorgeous with a make-up bag filled with sinfully expensive cosmetics. Birthdays can be positively embraced with a card promoting the benefits of cake and an album for all your gorgeous photographs. Two pillow signs will bring a touch of glamour with bright pink feather and sequin trims, while a glasses case shows that getting older doesn't mean we can't continue to have fun.

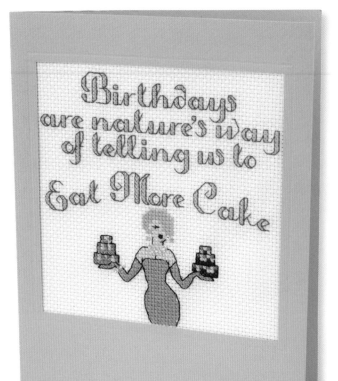

Put a positive spin on getting older with this fun birthday card – perfect for a friend who is still in their prime, and determined to remain that way.

So you're getting older...so you need glasses...so what – have fun and be outrageous with a glasses case and fabulous sequined pillow sign.

Photo Album

The design on this smart photo album is quick to stitch but with a touch of glamour. There are many albums available from high street stores and this design will need one at least 23cm (9in) square.

STITCH COUNT
68h x 60w
DESIGN SIZE
12.5 x 11cm (5 x 4¼in)
MATERIALS
*   White 14-count Aida 23 x 21.5cm (9 x 8½in)
*   Tapestry needle size 24
*   DMC stranded cotton (floss) as listed in chart key
*   Mill Hill seed beads in silver
*   Medium-weight iron-on interfacing the same size as the Aida fabric
*   Felt 20 x 20cm (8 x 8in) to tone with stitching
*   Purchased photo album
*   Double-sided adhesive tape

1   Prepare for work (see page 98). Mark the centre of the fabric and centre of the chart on page 17. Use an embroidery frame if you wish.

2   Start stitching from the centre of the chart and fabric, using two strands of stranded cotton (floss) for full and three-quarter cross stitch and one strand for backstitch. Using matching thread, attach the beads where shown on the chart (see also the box below).

3   Once all stitching is complete, make up into a patch as follows. Fuse the iron-on interfacing to the wrong side of the embroidery according to the manufacturer's instructions. Trim the Aida to within eight blocks of the embroidery all round. Fold six blocks to the back all round and tack (baste) into place. Pin and tack the patch into place on the felt and sew around all sides. Remove tacking and trim the felt to within 1cm (³⁄8in) of the embroidery. Finish by using double-sided tape to stick the patch to the album.

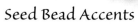

Seed Bead Accents
Using beads in a design adds interest and texture, and in this chapter they also bring a touch of glamour and sparkle. You could change the bead colour if desired. Attach beads with a beading needle, which is longer and thinner than a tapestry needle and will pass through the tiny hole in the seed bead. Use matching thread and refer to the diagram on page 100.

Glasses Case

STITCH COUNT
50h x 80w

DESIGN SIZE
9 x 14.5cm (3½ x 5¾in)

MATERIALS
* White 14-count Aida 19 x 25.5cm (7½ x 10in)
* Tapestry needle size 24
* DMC stranded cotton (floss) as listed in chart key
* Fabric for case, one piece 14 x 21cm (5½ x 8¼in) and one piece 25.5 x 21cm (10 x 8¼in)
* Thin wadding (batting) 25.5 x 21cm (10 x 8¼in)

This wry sentiment is perfect to adorn a case for glasses. The case is really easy to make and you could use the same idea to create a mobile phone holder.

1 Prepare for work (see page 98). Mark the centre of the fabric and centre of the chart on page 13. Use an embroidery frame if you wish.

2 Start stitching from the centre of the chart and fabric, using two strands of stranded cotton (floss) for full and three-quarter cross stitch and one strand for backstitch.

3 Once all stitching is complete, make up into a case as follows. Trim the embroidery to 14cm (5½in) high and 21cm (8¼in) wide, making sure the design is in the centre. With right sides facing, place the embroidery and smaller fabric piece together. Using a 1.3cm (½in) seam allowance, sew around three edges, leaving one short edge open. Turn through to the right side and press, pushing out corners. Turn 1.3cm (½in) to the wrong side around the open edge and tack (baste) in place.

4 To make a lining, fold the larger fabric piece in half to make a piece 12.5cm (5in) deep. Sew around two sides, leaving one short edge open. Turn 1.3cm (½in) to the wrong side around the open edge and tack (baste) in place. Wrap the piece of wadding (batting) around the lining, matching raw edges. Tack the wadding in place, working next to the stitching line in the lining's seam allowance. With wrong sides facing, insert the lining and wadding into the outer case, matching side seams. Slip stitch the lining to the outer case around the open edge and remove tacking when finished.

Birthday Card

STITCH COUNT
67h x 67w

DESIGN SIZE
12.2 x 12.2cm (4¾ x 4¾in)

A cake in each hand is the perfect way to enjoy a balanced diet on a girl's birthday (see page 6). Use the chart on page 16 and stitch the design on a 18cm (7in) square of white 14-count Aida, using two strands for cross stitch and one for backstitch. Using matching thread, sew on the silver beads as on the chart. Mount the design in a double-fold card with a 12.5cm (5in) square aperture (see page 101).

Pillow Hangings

Two fabulous stuffed pillow hangings make great gifts for friends and family.

STITCH COUNTS
Feather Pillow 96h x 54w
Sequin Pillow 107h x 75w
DESIGN SIZES
Feather Pillow 17.5 x 10cm (7 x 4in)
Sequin Pillow 19.5 x 13.6cm (7¾ x 5½in)
MATERIALS (for each pillow)
*   White 14-count Aida 30.5 x 23cm (12 x 9in)
*   Tapestry needle size 24
*   DMC stranded cotton (floss) as listed
    in chart key
*   Backing fabric same size as Aida
*   Polyester toy stuffing
*   Feather boa trim or sequin braid trim
    100cm (40in) long
*   Piping cord 23cm (9in) long

1 Prepare for work (see page 98). Mark the centre of the fabric and centre of the chart on page 14 or 15. Use an embroidery frame if you wish.

2 Start stitching from the centre of the chart and fabric, using two strands of stranded cotton (floss) for full and three-quarter cross stitch and one strand for backstitch.

3 Once all stitching is complete, make up into a pillow sign as follows. Place pins to mark either side of the finished embroidery at the widest part, and at top and bottom at the widest part. Measure 4cm (1½in) from these markers and trim the embroidery to size, following a line of squares for a straight edge. Cut the backing fabric to the same size.

4 With right sides facing, place the embroidery and backing fabric together. Using a 1.3cm (½in) seam allowance, sew around three edges, leaving the lower edge open. Turn through to the right side and press, pushing out the corners. Turn 1.3cm (½in) to the wrong side around the open edge and press. Stuff the pillow, pushing the stuffing into the corners. Slip stitch the open edge closed.

5 Make a hanging loop by sewing each end of the piping cord to the wrong side at the top edge 2.5cm (1in) in from the side edges. Sew the feather or sequin trim around the pillow along the seam line. When sewing on a feather trim, to avoid pulling feathers through with the needle, use large over-stitches, putting the needle through the fabric from front to back and then taking over the feathers and through the fabric from front to back again. Pull up tight and continue around the edges. After finishing, release any feathers caught in the stitches.

Fabulously over the top, this hanging sign will warn everyone you are on top form. This pillow is edged with a delicious pink feather boa trim, while the one shown on page 7 uses a lovely sequin trimming.

I don't have
hot flushes;
I have
Power Surges

Make-up Bag

Ooze confidence no matter what your age with this simple statement. Sew the stitched patch to a ready-made make-up bag.

STITCH COUNT
64h x 79w
DESIGN SIZE
11.6 x 14.3cm (4½ x 5¾in)
MATERIALS
* White 14-count Aida 20 x 25.5cm (8 x 10in)
* Tapestry needle size 24
* DMC stranded cotton (floss) as listed in chart key
* Medium-weight iron-on interfacing the same size as Aida
* Ready-made make-up bag

1 Prepare for work (see page 98). Mark the centre of the fabric and centre of the chart opposite. Use an embroidery frame if you wish.

2 Start stitching from the centre of chart and fabric, using two strands of stranded cotton (floss) for full and three-quarter cross stitch and one strand for backstitch.

3 Once all stitching is complete, make up into a patch as follows. Fuse iron-on interfacing to the wrong side of the embroidery. Use pins to mark either side of the embroidery at the widest part, and the top and bottom widest part. Measure 1.3cm (½in) from these markers and trim the embroidery to size, following a line of squares for a straight edge. Turn raw edges to the wrong side, leaving two empty Aida squares around the embroidery. Tack (baste) the turnings into place.

4 To complete the project, sew the patch on to the ready-made make-up bag and remove the tacking.

Make-up Bag

DMC stranded cotton

Cross stitch

	210
	310
	321
	948

Backstitch

—— 718
—— 3371

So many birthdays
– yet still

So Beautiful

Young At Heart

older in other places

Glasses Case

DMC stranded cotton

Cross stitch

210	321	V 605	3806	/ blanc	
310	602	948	3821		

Backstitch

—— 718
—— 3371

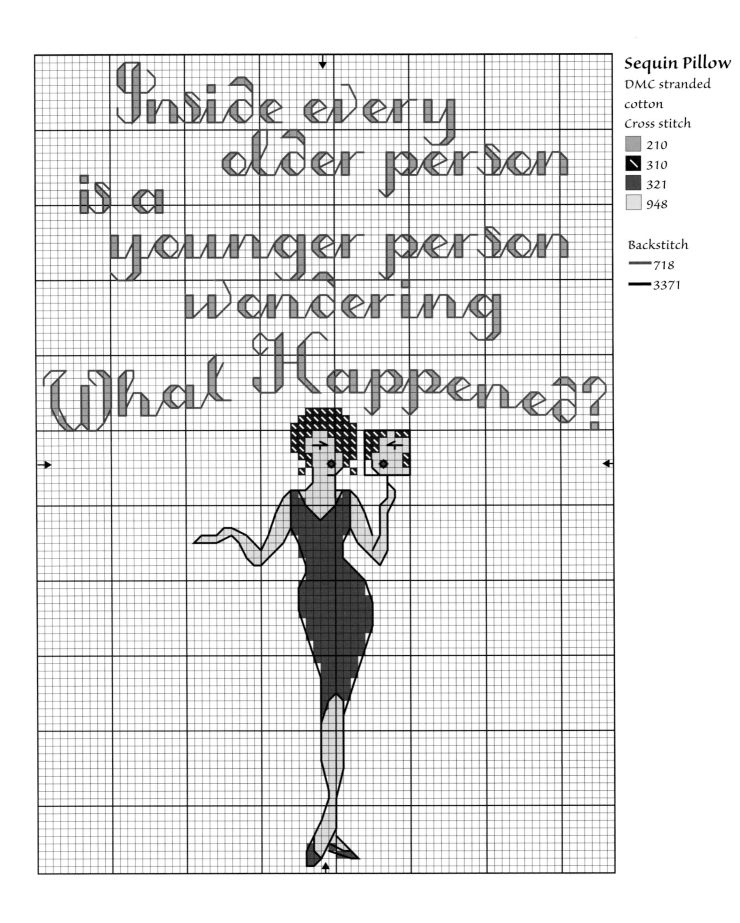

Sequin Pillow

DMC stranded cotton

Cross stitch

▨	210
◆	310
■	321
▨	948

Backstitch

—	718
—	3371

Feather Pillow

DMC stranded cotton

Cross stitch

▨	210
▨	321
⊡	602
V	605
▨	948
▨	955
▨	3806
▨	3821

Backstitch

──	718
──	3371

Ageing Disgracefully **15**

Birthday Card

DMC stranded cotton

Cross stitch

▣ 210	▣ 602	▣ 948	✕ 3064	▣ 3821
■ 321	✓ 605	▣ 955	▣ 3806	◉ 3857

Backstitch

— 718
— 3371

Mill Hill seed beads

⬤ 02010 silver

Photo Album

DMC stranded cotton

Cross stitch

210	550	3821
321	948	

Backstitch

— 718
— 3371

Mill Hill seed beads

 02010 silver

Work Woes

Work – now that's certainly a four letter word! Another eight hours of nonsense and tiresome colleagues to be endured before you can escape to freedom at 5pm. These ever-so-naughty designs will tell everyone in the office to leave you alone because you're really, really stressed and you really, really don't need any more work!

These six projects will add humour to your work space so that you can take it all in your stride. Make a sign to warn people off – with this on show how could they even think about giving you more work! A cute sleeping computer buddy will keep your unused PC company. Add witty remarks to customize your desk diary, pen holder and CD storage box. Finally, there's a mug jacket to keep your endless supply of coffee warm.

Keep your coffee or tea hot and remind your work colleagues how terrific you are with this handy mug jacket – see page 23.

Getting through the working day will be much easier with these witty sentiments to keep you going. The designs are made up as patches and can be used to adorn all sorts of work items.

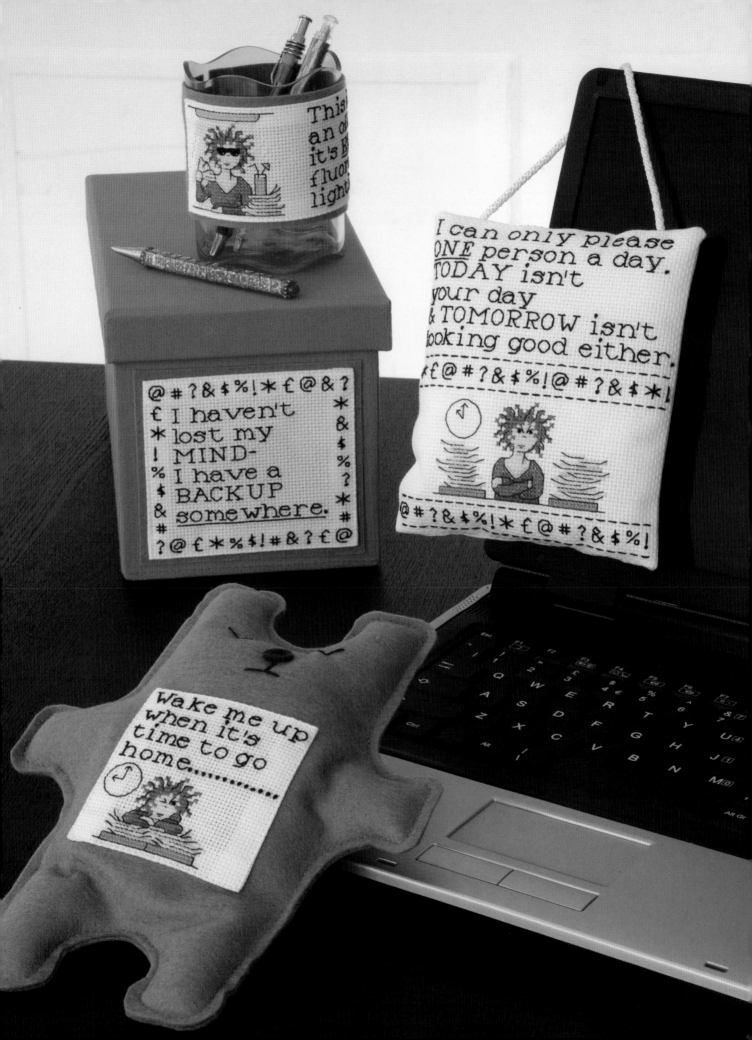

Computer Buddy

This cute toy is very easy to make and the design could be replaced with other sentiments. You could change the look of the buddy by using coloured or patterned felt – see also the car buddy on page 94.

STITCH COUNT
51h x 46w
DESIGN SIZE
8 x 7.3cm (3⅛ x 2¾in)
MATERIALS
* White 16-count Aida 18 x 18cm (7 x 7in)
* Tapestry needle size 24
* DMC stranded cotton (floss) as listed in chart key
* Felt, two pieces 30.5 x 25.5cm (12 x 10in)
* Tracing paper
* Polyester toy stuffing
* One button

1 Prepare for work (see page 98). Mark the centre of the fabric and centre of the chart on page 26. Use an embroidery frame if you wish.

2 Start stitching from the centre of the chart and fabric, using two strands of stranded cotton (floss) for cross stitch, French knots and backstitch writing and one strand for backstitch outlines. Once stitching is complete, make up as a patch as in step 3 of the make-up bag on page 12.

3 Make a buddy as follows. Using tracing paper, draw around the pattern on page 103 and mark the face details. Cut out the pattern piece. Place the two pieces of felt together and pin the pattern on top. Cut the felt around the pattern and then remove the pins.

4 Place the pattern on to one felt piece and use four strands of black stranded cotton to sew the face details through the tracing paper. Sew on the button for a nose and then remove the pattern by carefully tearing around the stitches and button.

5 Place the embroidered patch on to the front piece of felt, centrally, with the top edge in line with the top of the arms. Pin and tack (baste) in place and then sew around all four sides. With wrong sides facing, place the two felt pieces together, matching edges carefully and pin and tack (baste) in place. Using a 6mm (¼in) seam, stitch around the edge of the felt pieces, leaving a 5cm (2in) gap along the straight edge at one side. Remove tacking and stuff the buddy, pushing the stuffing into the arms, legs and ears. Sew the open edge closed to finish.

Work Pillow Sign

Work – there's always too much to do and too little time to do it. This sassy warning may keep people at bay, at least for a while.

STITCH COUNT
83h x 73w
DESIGN SIZE
15 x 13.3cm (6 x 5¼in)
MATERIALS
* White 14-count Aida 25.5 x 23cm (10 x 9in)
* Tapestry needle size 24
* DMC stranded cotton (floss) as listed in chart key
* Piece of backing fabric same size as Aida
* Polyester toy stuffing
* Piping cord 23cm (9in) long

1 Prepare for work (see page 98). Mark the centre of the fabric and centre of the chart on page 25. Use an embroidery frame if you wish.

2 Start stitching from the centre of the chart and fabric, using two strands of stranded cotton (floss) for full and three-quarter cross stitch, French knots and backstitch writing and one strand for backstitch outlines.

3 Once all stitching is complete, make up into a pillow sign as follows. Place pins to mark either side of the finished embroidery at the widest part, and also at top and bottom at the widest part. Measure 2cm (¾in) from these markers and trim the embroidery to size, following a line of Aida squares for a straight edge. Cut the backing fabric to the same size.

4 With right sides facing, place the embroidery and backing fabric together. Using a 1.3cm (½in) seam allowance, sew around three edges, leaving the lower edge open. Turn through to the right side and press, pushing out the corners. Turn 1.3cm (½in) to the wrong side around the open edge and press. Stuff the pillow, pushing the stuffing into the corners. Slip stitch the open edge closed.

5 To finish the pillow sign, make a hanging loop by sewing each end of the piping cord to the wrong side at the top edge 2.5cm (1in) in from the side edges.

Desk Diary

Customizing your diary with this fun design couldn't be easier and making the design into a patch means you can use it to decorate other items, such as a notebook or pencil case.

1 Prepare for work (see page 98). Mark the centre of the fabric and centre of the chart on page 26. Use an embroidery frame if you wish.

2 Start stitching from the centre of the chart and fabric, using two strands of stranded cotton (floss) for full and three-quarter cross stitch, two strands for French knots and backstitch writing and one strand for backstitch outlines. Once all stitching is complete, make up into a patch following step 3 of the make-up bag on page 12.

3 Pin and tack (baste) the patch into place in the centre of the felt and sew around all four sides. Trim the felt to within 6mm (¼in) of the Aida.

4 On the wrong side of the felt, stick double-sided tape around the edges and peel off backing tape. Finish by sticking the patch on to the front of diary.

STITCH COUNT
57h x 53w
DESIGN SIZE
10.3 x 9.6cm (4 x 3¾in)
MATERIALS
* White 14-count Aida 20 x 20cm (8 x 8in)
* Tapestry needle size 24
* DMC stranded cotton (floss) as listed in chart key
* Felt 18 x 18cm (7 x 7in)
* Diary approximately 20 x 15cm (8 x 6in)
* Double-sided adhesive tape

Work Mates

A jacket to keep your coffee or tea warm is a must to get through a day at the office, while a pen pot is handy to rummage in and look busy when the boss is around. The jackets are made in the same way.

STITCH COUNTS
Coffee Mug 24h x 98w
Pen Holder 30h x 90w
DESIGN SIZES
Coffee Mug 4.4 x 18cm (1¾ x 7in)
Pen Holder 5.5 x 16.5cm (2⅛ x 6½in)
MATERIALS (for each project)
*   White 14-count Aida: for coffee mug 14.5 x 28cm (6 x 11in); for pen holder 15 x 25cm (6 x 10in)
*   Tapestry needle size 24
*   DMC stranded cotton (floss) as listed in chart key
*   Felt for coffee mug 10 x 30cm (4 x 12in); for pen holder 12 x 30cm (5 x 12in)
*   Two buttons
*   Elastic 1.3cm (½in) wide x 15cm (6in) long
*   Mug with straight sides or a pen holder

1   Prepare for work (see page 98). Mark the centre of the fabric and centre of the chart on page 27.

2   Start stitching from the centre of the chart and fabric, using two strands of stranded cotton (floss) for full and three-quarter cross stitch. Stitch DMC 727 (yellow) as half cross stitch. Use two strands for French knots and backstitch writing and one strand for backstitch outlines.

3   Once stitching is complete, make up as a patch as in step 3 on page 12. Pin and tack (baste) the patch in place in the centre of the felt and sew around all four sides. Trim the felt to within 6mm (¼in) of the Aida along the top edges only.

4   To make the coffee mug jacket, wrap the jacket around the mug and measure the length needed, leaving a gap between the two ends for the handle. Trim off excess felt. Sew the buttons into the corners of one end, 1.3cm (½in) from the edge. Cut the elastic in half. Make a buttonhole in the centre of one end of each piece 6mm (¼in) from the edge and then put the buttons through the buttonholes. Wrap the jacket around the container and stretch the elastic from the button to meet the other end. Pull the elastic though the handle or put one piece over the handle if the gap is too small. Measure the length of elastic needed, trim off excess and sew the ends of the elastic to the felt. Wrap the jacket around the container and fasten.

5   To make the pen holder jacket, wrap the jacket around the pen holder and measure the length needed so the ends butt up against each other with no overlap. Trim off any excess felt. Make up the pen pot jacket as above.

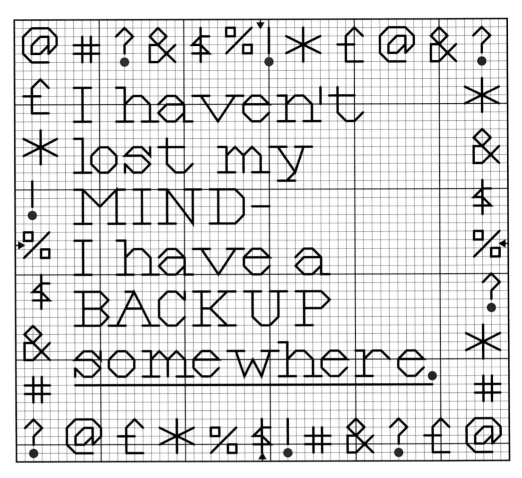

CD Box

DMC stranded cotton

Backstitch

— 310 (2 strands)

French knots

● 310

CD Box

- STITCH COUNT
- 51h x 56w
- DESIGN SIZE
- 9.3 x 10cm (3¾ x 4in)

This amusing design is quick to stitch and would make a great gift for an office colleague. CD boxes are available from high street stores. Use the chart here and stitch the design on a 20 x 20cm (8 x 8in) piece of white 14-count Aida, using two strands for cross stitch, French knots and backstitch. Back the embroidery with iron-on interfacing, trim to size and use double-sided tape to stick the patch to a 15cm (6in) square of felt. To finish, trim the felt to within 6mm (¼in) of the Aida and stick the mounted patch on to your CD box.

Work Pillow Sign

DMC stranded cotton

Cross stitch

- ■ 304
- ■ 644
- \ 754
- □ 948
- ■ 602
- O 666
- V 920
- + ecru

Backstitch

— 310 (2 strands for writing and 1 strand for outlines)

French knots

● 310

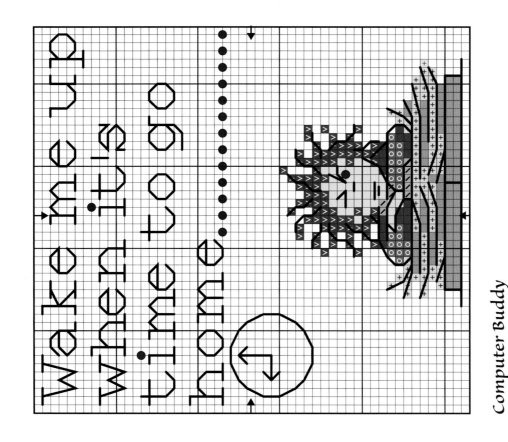

Computer Buddy

DMC stranded cotton

Cross stitch

■ 304	╱ 754
▨ 602	▼ 920
▨ 644	948
⊙ 666	+ ecru

Backstitch

—— 310 (2 strands
for writing and
1 strand for outlines)

French knots

● 310

Desk Diary

DMC stranded cotton

Cross stitch

■ 304	▨ 644	▼ 920
▨ 602	⊙ 666	948
╱ 604	╱ 754	+ ecru

Backstitch

—— 310 (2 strands for
writing and 1 strand
for outlines)

French knots

● 310

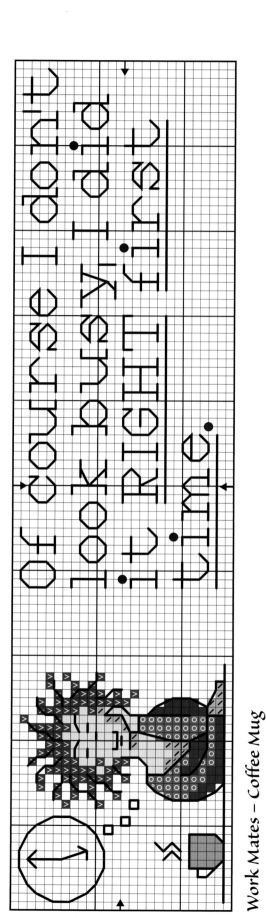

Work Mates – Coffee Mug

DMC stranded cotton

Cross stitch

	304		666		920
	602		754		948

Backstitch

— 310 (use 2 strands for writing and 1 strand for outlines)

French knots

● 310

Work Mates – Pen Pot

DMC stranded cotton

Cross stitch

	304	−	741
	310	/	754
	602	V	920
	644		948
O	666	•	972
	727 (half cross stitch)	+	ecru

Backstitch

— 310 (use 2 strands for writing and 1 strand for outlines)

French knots

● 310

Born to Shop

It's hard to believe but there are some people who don't understand the thrill of shopping – all you can do is pity them. You know the value of retail therapy, that wonderful satisfaction to be gained from buying one more pair of shoes, or another handbag, a dress, or jewellery, or more of anything really.

If only you could spend all day shopping – what bliss!

Here are six coordinating projects to celebrate this most worthwhile occupation. The designs are quick to stitch so you can add a message to almost anything – a handbag, a credit card wallet or a mobile phone case. For the shoe addict there's a traditional-style sampler and a notebook cover. And even though your wardrobe may be bursting, the message on a little pillow sign will have you nodding in agreement.

This mobile phone holder is really easy to make and some shiny seed beads add a pretty finishing touch.

The matching designs in this chapter celebrate that most satisfying occupation – shopping! It's so easy to customize a handbag, a notebook or a wallet – perfect for trips to the shops.

Handbag

Preparing this embroidered design as a patch means that it can be sewn or glued to almost any type of handbag (see page 29).

STITCH COUNT
80h x 86w

DESIGN SIZE
14.5 x 15.6cm (5¾ x 6⅛in)

MATERIALS
* Cream 14-count Aida 25.5 x 25.5cm (10 x 10in)
* Tapestry needle size 24
* DMC stranded cotton (floss) as listed in chart key
* Mill Hill beads as listed in chart key
* Medium-weight iron-on interfacing the same size as the Aida
* Bias binding 1.3cm (½in) wide x 80cm (32in) long
* Purchased handbag

1 Prepare for work (see page 98). Mark the centre of the fabric and chart on page 36. Use an embroidery frame if you wish.

2 Start stitching from the centre of the chart and fabric, using two strands of stranded cotton (floss) for full and three-quarter cross stitch and one strand for backstitch. Using matching thread, attach the beads where shown on the chart.

3 Once all stitching is complete, make up into a patch as follows. Fuse the iron-on interfacing to the wrong side of the embroidery according to the manufacturer's instructions. Trim the embroidery to size, leaving six empty squares of Aida on all sides.

4 Fold the bias binding in half and press. Sew the binding along the top edge of the Aida, covering the raw edge. Trim the ends of the bias binding level with the Aida edge. Repeat for the lower edge, then for each side. To finish, sew on to the front of your bag.

Shopping Pillow Sign

Make this pillow sign for a shopaholic friend to hang on their wardrobe or closet. Use the chart on page 37 and stitch the design on a 23 x 23cm (9 x 9in) piece of cream 14-count Aida. Use two strands of thread for full and three-quarter cross stitch and one strand for backstitch. Sew on the beads where shown on the chart. Using a piece of backing fabric the same size as the Aida, make up into a pillow sign following steps 3–5 on page 21 using a 23cm (9in) length of piping cord for a handle.

STITCH COUNT
71h x 69w

DESIGN SIZE
12.8 x 12.8cm (5 x 5in)

Mobile Phone Cover

A mobile phone cover makes a great gift – either make your own cover or sew the embroidered patch on to a ready-made one. Felt has been used to line the cover and you could choose a different colour for the outside.

STITCH COUNT
54h x 38w
DESIGN SIZE
10 x 7cm (4 x 2¾in)
MATERIALS
* Cream 14-count Aida 20 x 18cm (8 x 7in)
* Tapestry needle size 24
* DMC stranded cotton (floss) as listed in chart key
* Mill Hill beads as listed in chart key
* Medium-weight iron-on interfacing the same size as the Aida
* Two pieces of felt (one for lining) each 9 x 25.5cm (3½ x 10in)
* One button
* Ribbon 1cm (³/₈in) wide x 12.7cm (5in) long

1 Prepare for work (see page 98). Mark the centre of the fabric and centre of the chart on page 39. Use an embroidery frame if you wish.

2 Start stitching from the centre of the chart and fabric, using two strands of stranded cotton (floss) for full and three-quarter cross stitch and one strand for backstitch. Using matching thread, attach the beads where shown on the chart. Once all stitching is complete, make up into a patch following step 3 for the make-up bag on page 12.

3 Sew the patch on to a ready-made phone cover or make a cover as follows. On one felt piece, place the patch 6mm (¼in) from the top edge. Pin and tack (baste) in position then sew around all four sides.

4 Place the two felt pieces together, patch on the outside, and pin around the edges. Fold the ribbon in half and sandwich it between the two layers at centre top above the patch. Tack (baste) around all edges. Topstitch across each short end 6mm (¼in) from the edge. Fold the cover in half and topstitch the two side seams 6mm (¼in) from the edge. Remove all tacking (basting). Fold the ribbon loop over to the back and mark the position of the button. Sew on the button to finish.

This wallet is easy to make or you could sew or glue the embroidered patch on to a ready-made wallet. The felt used as a lining could be in a contrasting colour to that used for the outside.

STITCH COUNT
72h x 50w
DESIGN SIZE
11.5 x 8cm (4½ x 3⅛in)
MATERIALS
* Cream 16-count Aida 21.5 x 18cm (8½ x 7in)
* Tapestry needle size 24
* DMC stranded cotton (floss) as listed in chart key
* Medium-weight iron-on interfacing the same size as the Aida
* Felt for the wallet 9 x 24cm (3½ x 9½in)
* Two pieces of felt (one for lining) each 10 x 26cm (4 x 10¼in)
* Two pieces of felt each 10cm (4in) square, to match outer felt piece
* One button
* Ribbon 1cm (³⁄₈in) wide x 12.7cm (5in) long

1 Prepare for work (see page 98). Mark the centre of the fabric and chart on page 39. Use an embroidery frame if you wish.

2 Start stitching from the centre of the chart and fabric, using two strands of stranded cotton (floss) for full and three-quarter cross stitch and one strand for backstitch. Once all stitching is complete, make up into a patch following step 3 for the make-up bag on page 12.

3 Sew the patch on to a ready-made wallet or make a wallet as follows. On the large felt piece to be used for the outer, place the patch 6mm (¼in) from the top edge. Pin and tack (baste) in position, then sew around all four sides. On the lining felt piece, place a small felt piece at each end, matching edges. Tack in place along three sides, leaving the open edges facing the middle, to form two pockets. Sew each pocket around three sides 1cm (³⁄₈in) from the edge.

4 With wrong sides facing, place the two felt pieces together and pin around the edges. Fold the ribbon in half and sandwich it between the two layers at centre top above the patch. Tack (baste) around all edges. Topstitch around all edges 6mm (¼in) from the edge. Remove all tacking (basting). Fold the ribbon loop over to the back and mark the position of the button. Sew on the button to finish.

Home Sweet Home Picture

Any of the designs in this chapter would make attractive framed pictures and high
street stores have plenty of ready-made frames to choose from.

STITCH COUNT
82h x 109w
DESIGN SIZE
15 x 19.8cm (6 x 7¾in)
MATERIALS
* Cream 14-count Aida 25.5 x 30.5cm (10 x 12in)
* Tapestry needle size 24
* DMC stranded cotton (floss) as listed in chart key
* Picture frame to fit embroidery
* Mount board
* Thin wadding (batting)
* Double-sided adhesive tape

1 Prepare for work (see page 98). Mark the centre of the fabric
and chart on page 38. Use an embroidery frame if you wish.

2 Start stitching from the centre of the chart and fabric, using two
strands of stranded cotton (floss) for full and three-quarter cross
stitch and one strand for backstitch.

3 Once all stitching is complete, make up into a framed picture as
described on page 102.

For this sentiment a simple natural-coloured wooden
frame has been used but you could paint the frame to
echo one of the colours in the design.

HOME SWEET HOME
is where
I keep my shoes
while I'm out
buying more shoes

Notebook Cover

Small notebooks are so useful and make a quick gift for a friend or family member – perfect for notes about the latest purchases and the best shops to visit!

1. Prepare for work (see page 98). Mark the centre of the fabric and centre of the chart opposite. Use an embroidery frame if you wish.

2. Start stitching from the centre of the chart and fabric, using two strands of stranded cotton (floss) for full and three-quarter cross stitch and one strand for backstitch. Once all stitching is complete, make up into a patch following step 3 for the make-up bag on page 12.

3. Wrap the piece of felt around the notebook, turning the excess at each side over the cover to the back. Place the embroidery on the front so it is centralized and pin in position. Remove the notebook. Cut the ribbon in half and tuck one end under the patch in the middle. Tack (baste) in position, catching the ribbon into the stitches. Sew the patch in place.

4. Wrap the felt around the notebook, again turning the excess at each side over the cover to the back. Pin these turnings along the top and bottom edges. Tack (baste) in place. To secure the turnings, topstitch along the top and bottom edges about 6mm (¼in) from the edge.

5. Sew the other piece of ribbon to the back to match the one on the front. Insert the notebook and tie the ribbon in a bow to finish.

STITCH COUNT
64h x 70w
DESIGN SIZE
11.6 x 12.7cm (4½ x 5in)
MATERIALS
* Cream 14-count Aida 20 x 23cm (8 x 9in)
* Tapestry needle size 24
* DMC stranded cotton (floss) as listed in chart key
* Medium-weight iron-on interfacing the same size as the Aida
* Felt 23.5 x 80cm (9¼ x 32in)
* Narrow ribbon 46cm (18in) long
* A5 notebook 21 x 15cm (8¼ x 6in)

Notebook Cover

DMC stranded cotton

Cross stitch

	166		316	⟍ 3042
O	315	V	779	

Backstitch

—— 3371

Handbag

DMC stranded cotton

Cross stitch

▨ 166	⊙ 315	ⱽ 779
⊡ 310	▨ 316	⬲ 3042

Backstitch

— 3371

Mill Hill seed beads

⬤ 00553 old rose

Shopping Pillow Sign

DMC stranded cotton

Cross stitch

	166		316		3042
O	315	V	779		

Backstitch

— 3371

Mill Hill seed beads

⬤ 00553 old rose

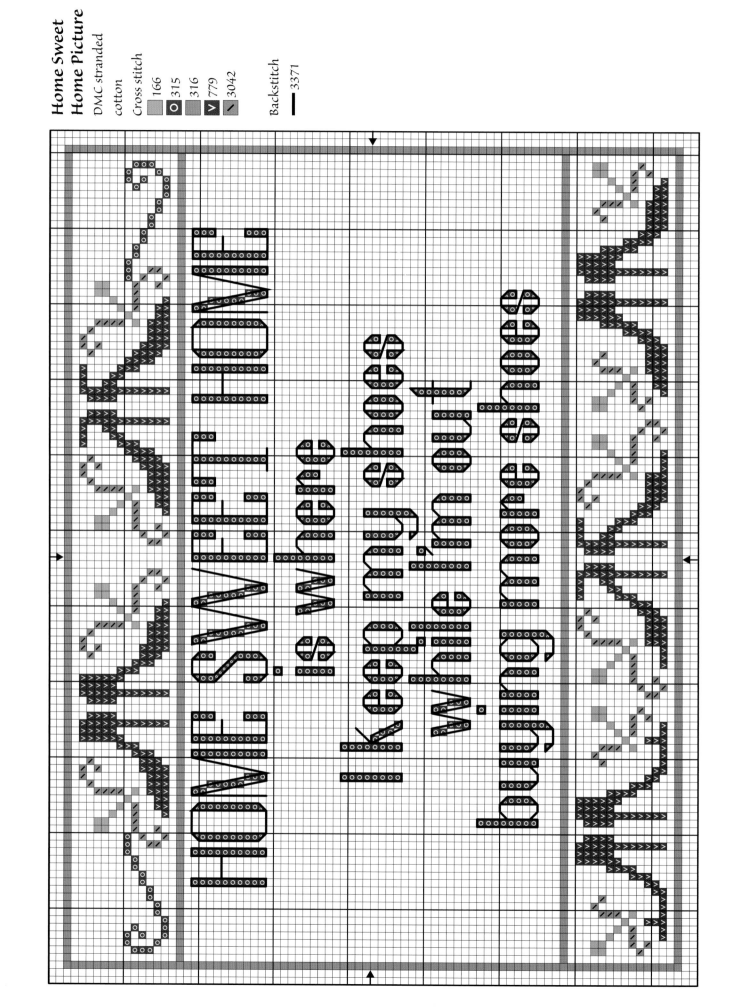

Mobile Phone Cover

DMC stranded cotton

Cross stitch		Backstitch
▦ 166		── 3371
⊙ 315		
▦ 316		
∨ 779		
◪ 3042		

Mill Hill seed beads

● 00553 old rose

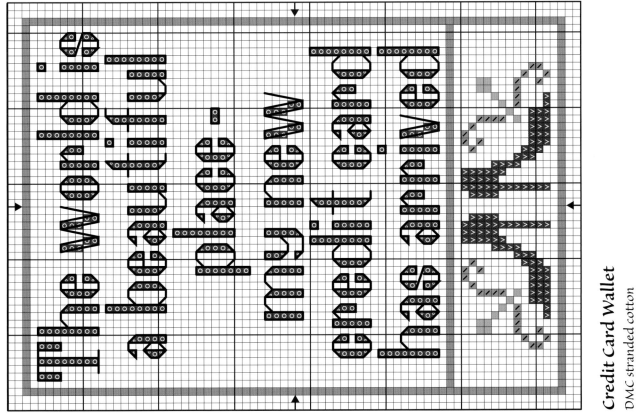

Credit Card Wallet

DMC stranded cotton

Cross stitch		Backstitch
▦ 166	◪ 3042	── 3371
⊙ 315		
▦ 316		
∨ 779		

Domestic Bliss

Was there ever a more futile occupation than housework? You do the dusting and vacuuming and a week later it needs doing all over again. There are the kitchen chores too – all that daily cooking and dreary washing up. So put your foot down and say no to all this domestic slavery – after all, a messy house may stop the in-laws visiting.

The amusing designs in this chapter put housework firmly in its place – last on your list of priorities! Three heart-shaped pillows edged with yellow gingham and embellished with daisy buttons carry encouraging reasons for not doing the cleaning. A coordinated tea towel and pot holder look too lovely to use and provide another excuse to avoid the cooking. And if all these don't get the message across, a framed picture proves you're just too perfect to do housework.

You can look at the dust, just don't write in it

Three bright, heart-shaped pillow hangings (see opposite and page 43) are not only really simple to make but will show everyone just what you think of housework.

The tongue-in-cheek designs in this chapter use a cheerful daisy and yellow gingham theme and warn family and friends that you are no domestic angel.

Housework
can't kill you–
but why take
the chance?

I'm a DOMESTIC ANGEL

if you ever see me cook

it'll be a MIRACLE

Domestic Angel Picture

This design makes a fun framed picture for the kitchen and could also be used as a patch on an apron.

STITCH COUNT
63h x 95w
DESIGN SIZE
11.5 x 17.3cm (4½ x 6¾in)
MATERIALS

* Cream 14-count Aida 21.5 x 28cm (8½ x 11in)
* Tapestry needle size 24
* DMC stranded cotton (floss) as listed in chart key
* Daisy buttons (optional): one 2.5cm (1in) diameter and two 2cm (¾in) diameter
* Frame to fit the embroidery
* Mount board
* Thin wadding (batting)
* Double-sided adhesive tape

1 Prepare for work (see page 98). Mark the centre of the fabric and centre of the chart on page 48. Use an embroidery frame if you wish.

2 Start stitching from the centre of the chart and fabric, using two strands of stranded cotton (floss) for cross stitches, one strand for pink backstitches and two strands for green backstitch and for the writing. If you want to replace the stitched daisies with daisy buttons refer to the box below.

3 Once all the stitching is complete, finish your picture by mounting and framing (see page 102).

Shaped Buttons
There are some wonderful buttons available today in all sorts of shapes, such as these bold daisies, which add just the right finishing touch to a project. If you choose to use buttons rather than cross stitching, sew the button in position on to the Aida where the centre of the stitched daisy is.

Heart Pillows

Little heart-shaped pillows are perfect for displaying some short and snappy sayings (see pages 40 and 41 for the other two hearts). Some gingham ribbon, decorative braid and a daisy button add pretty finishing touches.

STITCH COUNT (for each design)
55h x 55w
DESIGN SIZE
10 x 10cm (4 x 4in)
MATERIALS (for each heart)
* Cream 14-count Aida 20 x 20cm (8 x 8in)
* Tapestry needle size 24
* DMC stranded cotton (floss) as listed in chart key
* Daisy button 2cm (¾in) diameter (optional)
* Backing fabric the same size as the Aida
* Polyester toy stuffing
* Ribbon 2.5cm (1in) wide x 68cm (27in) long
* Daisy braid 1cm (³⁄₈in) wide x 16cm (6¼in) long

1 Prepare for work (see page 98). Mark the centre of the fabric and centre of the chart on page 46 or 47. Use an embroidery frame if you wish.

2 Start stitching from the centre of the chart and fabric, using two strands of stranded cotton (floss) for cross stitches, one strand for pink backstitches and two strands for green backstitch and for the writing. To replace the cross stitched daisies with daisy buttons refer to the box opposite.

3 Once all stitching is complete, make up into a heart-shaped pillow sign as follows. With right sides facing, place the embroidery and backing fabric together, with the embroidery on top. Sew around the heart shape keeping two Aida squares away from the outer stitches and leaving a 5cm (2in) gap in one of the straight edges. Turn through to the right side and press, pushing out the curved seams and the lower point. Turn the edges of the gap in by 1.3cm (½in) and press. Stuff the pillow, pushing the stuffing into the point. Slip stitch the open edge closed.

4 Make the frill as follows. Using strong thread, secure the end to one end of the ribbon and work a line of running stitches close to the edge for the entire length. Fold the ribbon in half and place a pin to mark the centre. Pin the frill around the heart behind the seam line on the backing fabric. Match the centre to the heart point and pull up the thread to gather the ribbon. Overlap the two ends at the centre top and sew the ribbon frill around the heart. Finish by making a hanging loop by folding the daisy braid in half and sewing it to the back at the top edge.

Pot Holder

Aida band is available in different widths, colours and with various decorative edges and is ideal for decorating ready-made items such as a pot holder or tea towel.

- STITCH COUNT
  24h x 105w
- DESIGN SIZE
  4.5 x 20cm (1¾ x 8in)
- MATERIALS
  * Aida band in cream (26 stitches wide) 30.5cm (12in) long x 5cm (2in) wide
  * Tapestry needle size 24
  * DMC stranded cotton (floss) as listed in chart key
  * Ready-made pot holder

1 Prepare for work (see page 98). Mark the centre of the Aida band and centre of the chart on page 49.

2 Start stitching from the centre of the chart and Aida band, using two strands of stranded cotton (floss) for cross stitches, one strand for pink backstitches and two strands for green backstitch and for the writing.

3 Once all stitching is complete, measure the width of the pot holder and trim the Aida band to size, adding 1.3cm (½in) at each end for turning under. Place the embroidery centrally and pin and tack (baste) the band into place on the pot holder, turning the raw ends under. Sew along all four sides to finish.

Tea Towel

- STITCH COUNT
  23h x 103w
- DESIGN SIZE
  4.5 x 20cm (1¾ x 8in)

This tea towel also uses Aida band and the design would also make a great bookmark for a recipe book. Work on cream Aida band (26 stitches wide) 60cm (24in) long x 5cm (2in) wide. Follow steps 1 and 2 above for stitching the design, using the chart on page 49. Measure the width of your tea towel and trim the Aida band to size, adding 1.5cm (½in) at each end for turning under. Position the embroidery centrally and tack (baste) the band into place on the towel, turning the raw ends under. Sew along all four sides to finish.

I only have a kitchen because it came with the house

Dinner is ready when the smoke alarm goes off

Heart Pillow 1

DMC stranded cotton

Cross stitch

☐ 726
■ 907
✓ blanc

Backstitch

— 433 (2 strands)
— 605 (1 strand)
— 907 (2 strands)

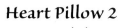

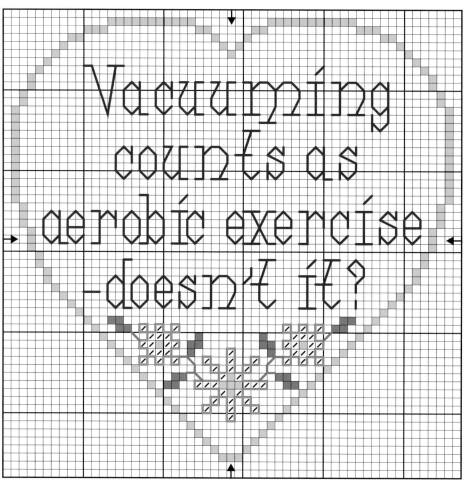

Heart Pillow 2

DMC stranded cotton

Cross stitch

☐ 726
■ 907
✓ blanc

Backstitch

— 433 (2 strands)
— 605 (1 strand)
— 907 (2 strands)

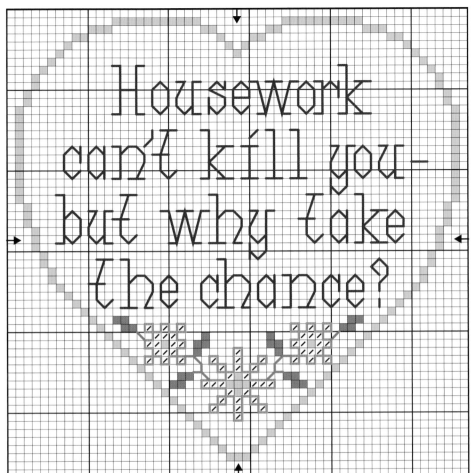

Heart Pillow 3

DMC stranded cotton

Cross stitch

▨	726
▉	907
✓	blanc

Backstitch

— 433 (2 strands)
— 605 (1 strand)
— 907 (2 strands)

If desired, a daisy button could replace the central stitched daisy on all of the projects featured in this chapter, as on the Heart Pillow shown right. To replace the cross stitched daisies with daisy buttons refer to the box on page 42.

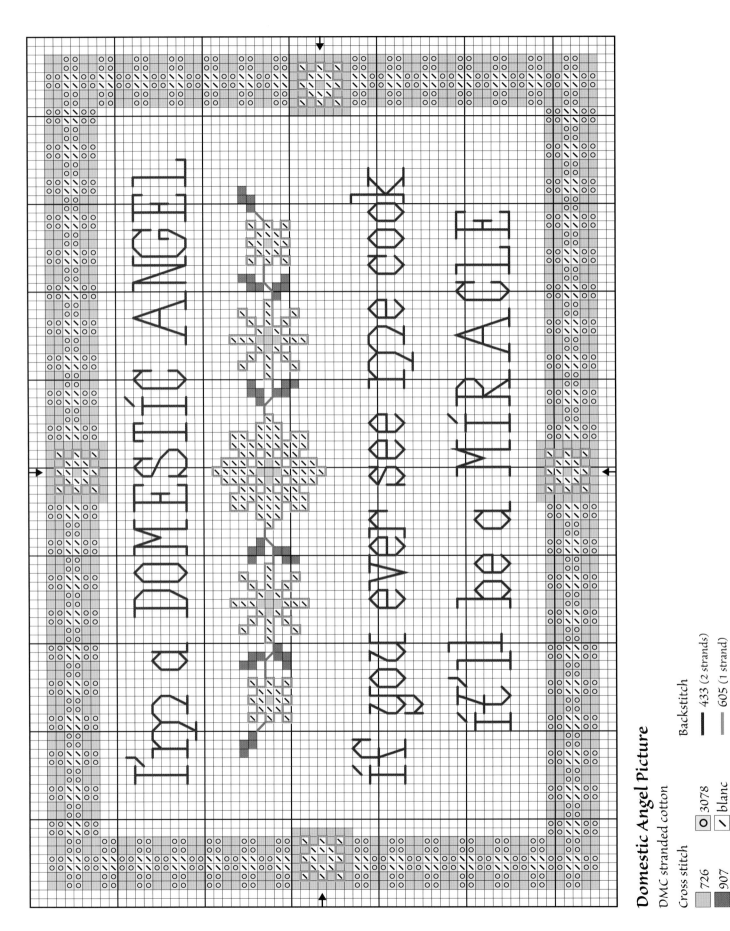

Domestic Angel Picture

DMC stranded cotton

Cross stitch

| 726 |
| 907 |

| ○ | 3078 |
| ✗ | blanc |

Backstitch

— 433 (2 strands)
— 605 (1 strand)
— 907 (2 strands)

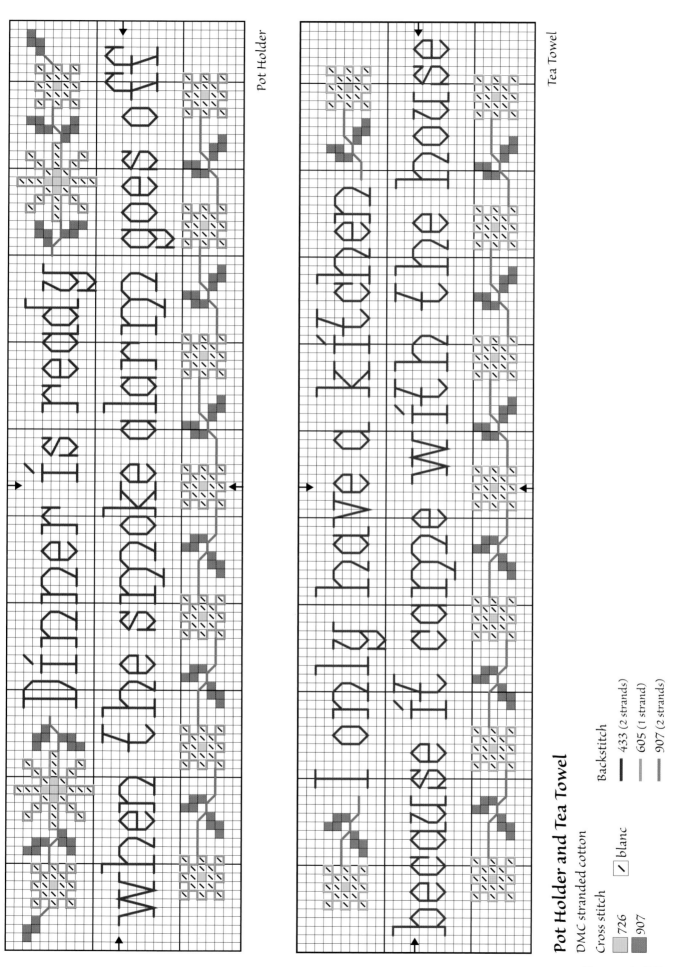

Pot Holder

Tea Towel

Pot Holder and Tea Towel

DMC stranded cotton

Cross stitch

	blanc
✓	726
	907

Backstitch

—— 433 (2 strands)
—— 605 (1 strand)
—— 907 (2 strands)

Domestic Bliss **49**

Christmas Chaos

If only we could buy our Christmas ready-made: presents would be selected and wrapped, cards written, the house cleaned, the decorations artfully arranged and all the food prepared. But no, it all has to be done and guess who has to do it – *you do!* Perhaps it should be called Stressmas!

The frazzled fairies on these four designs will allow you to express your own version of the Christmas spirit without resorting to 'Bah, humbug'! You could stitch a bright patch to decorate a gift bag and fill it with goodies for a special someone. Add a festive message to your calendar or send a Christmas card with chilly greetings, and if you really get desperate, send out a call for help with a Santa Stop Sign to greet visitors.

This design would be perfect to bring out with the Christmas decorations each year to remind the family that their help would be appreciated.

Ready-made items such as gift bags are ideal for displaying cross stitch embroidery and it's easy to customize a calendar too.

If Christmas is for Children,
why do WE have to be involved?

DECEMBER

	1	2	3	4	5	6
7	8	9	10	11	12	13
14						

MERRY
STRESSMAS

Gift Bag

Many stores sell gift bags in many sizes and colours so it will be easy to find one to suit this design (see page 51).

1 Prepare for work (see page 98). Mark the centre of the fabric and centre of the chart on page 56. Use an embroidery frame if you wish.

2 Start stitching from the centre of the chart and fabric, using two strands of stranded cotton (floss) for cross stitch and French knots, two strands for backstitch writing and one strand for other backstitch. Using matching thread, attach the beads where shown on the chart.

3 Once all stitching is complete, make up into a patch following step 3 for the make-up bag on page 12. Pin and tack (baste) the patch into place on the felt and sew around all four sides. Trim the felt to within 2.5cm (1in) of the embroidery. On the back of the felt, stick double-sided tape around the edges, peel off the backing tape and stick the patch to the bag.

Santa Stop Picture

Christmas is such a busy time for most of us that help is always welcome – and who better than Santa himself? (See picture on page 50.) Work on a 28 x 25.5cm (11 x 10in) piece of white 14-count Aida. Follow steps 1 and 2 above for stitching the design, using the chart on page 55. Make up into a framed picture (see page 102) and stick narrow ribbon to the back of the frame as a hanging loop.

Christmas Calendar

Turn a boring calendar into something special with this plaintive design. It could also be displayed as a pillow sign or as a framed picture to put in the kitchen at Christmas time.

STITCH COUNT
56h x 108w
DESIGN SIZE
10.2 x 19.5cm (4 x 7¾in)
MATERIALS
*   White 14-count Aida 20 x 30.5cm (8 x 12in)
*   Tapestry needle size 24
*   DMC stranded cotton (floss) and Light Effects thread as listed in chart key
*   Mill Hill beads as listed in chart key
*   Double-fold card with aperture to fit embroidery or thin card to make a card
*   December page from a calendar
*   Mount board
*   Narrow ribbon for hanger 25.5cm (10in)
*   Double-sided adhesive tape

1 Prepare for work, referring to page 98 if necessary. Mark the centre of the fabric and centre of the chart on page 57. Mount your fabric in an embroidery frame if you wish.

2 Start stitching from the centre of the chart and fabric, using two strands of stranded cotton (floss) for cross stitch, French knots and backstitch writing and one strand for other backstitch. Using matching thread, attach beads where shown on the chart. Once stitching is complete, mount into a double-fold card (see page 101).

3 If making your own aperture card, use thin card and draw a rectangle 26 x 48cm (10¼ x 18¾in) on it. Divide the width into three sections each 16cm (6³⁄₈in). Lightly score along the two lines separating the three sections to help folding. In the centre section draw lines 2cm (¾in) in from all four sides. Carefully cut along these lines to make the aperture. Fold in the left and right sections along the scored lines. Trim a small amount from the left edge so it lies flat when covering the back of the embroidery. Mount the embroidery into the card (see page 101).

4 Lay the calendar page with the embroidery card above it on the mount board. Mark the four corners and trim the mount board to size. Use double-sided tape to stick the calendar page on the mount board and to stick the ribbon in position for a hanging loop. Place the embroidery card over the top and stick in position.

Festive Card

DMC stranded cotton

Cross stitch

▓	321
∧	498
▓	904
▓	907
░	948
▓	3821
×	blanc
·	blanc + E5200 Light Effects (1 strand of each together in the needle)

Backstitch

— 498 (2 strands)

— 3371 (1 strand)

▭ blanc (2 strands)

French knots

● 3371

Mill Hill beads

◉ antique glass 03049 rich red

Festive Card

- **STITCH COUNT**
- 68h x 66w
- **DESIGN SIZE**
- 12.5 x 12cm (5 x 4¾in)

A grumpy fairy fed up with the winter weather creates a Christmas card with a difference. Use the chart above and stitch the design on a 23cm (9in) square of blue 14-count Aida. Use two strands of thread for cross stitch and French knots. Use two strands for backstitch writing, snowflakes and border and one strand for other backstitch. Sew on the beads in the positions shown on the chart. Use double-sided tape to mount the embroidery in a double-fold card with a 14.5cm (5½in) square aperture (see page 101).

Santa Stop Picture

DMC stranded cotton

Cross stitch

	151
	168
U	211
	321
	436
^	498
/	602
	907
	948
	3371
	3821
X	blanc
•	blanc + E5200 Light Effects (1 strand of each together in the needle)

Backstitch

——	498 (2 strands)
——	3371 (1 strand)

French knots

●	3371

Mill Hill beads

◉	antique glass 03049 rich red

Gift Bag

DMC stranded cotton
Cross stitch

■	321
◪	498
◹	729
■	904
⊙	906
◧	907
▨	948
■	3371
✕	blanc
⊡	blanc + E5200

Light Effects
(1 strand of each
together in the needle)

DMC Light Effects
Cross stitch

◹	E321
◹	E3821

Backstitch

——	498 (2 strands)
——	3371 (1 strand)

French knots

●	3371

Mill Hill beads

◉	antique glass 03049 rich red

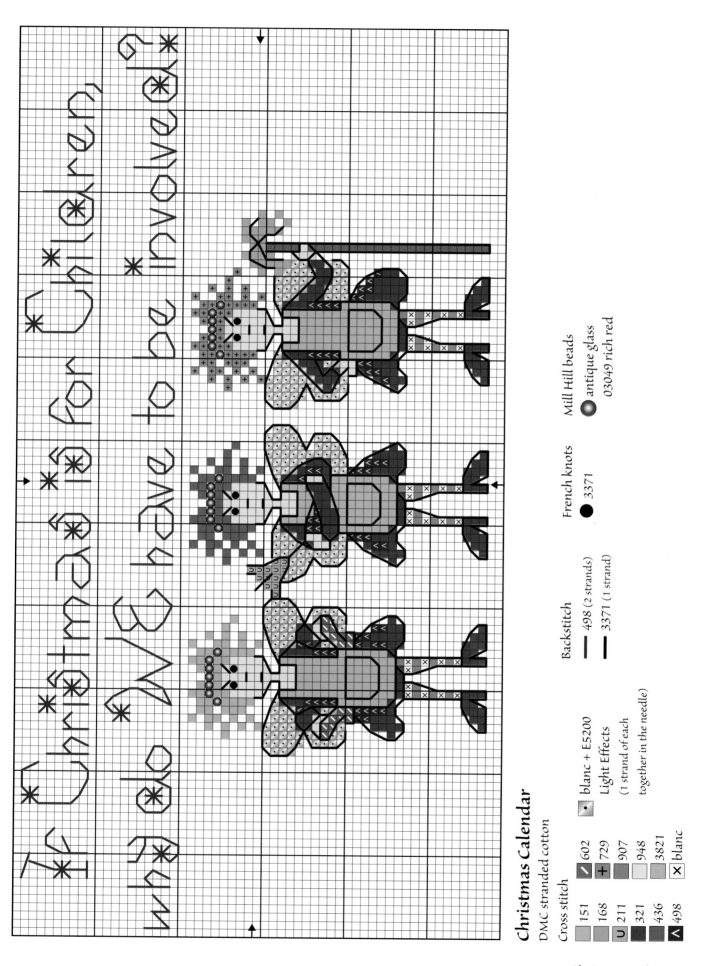

Christmas Calendar

DMC stranded cotton

Cross stitch

▨	151
◪	602
+	168
U	729
▦	211
▨	907
▨	321
▨	948
◪	436
▨	3821
◀	498
✕	blanc

▨	blanc + E5200
	Light Effects
	(1 strand of each
	together in the needle)

Backstitch

—— 498 (2 strands)

—— 3371 (1 strand)

French knots

● 3371

Mill Hill beads

◉ antique glass
03049 rich red

Food for Thought

Every day there seems to be news about a fabulous new diet, or something that you should or shouldn't be eating. Perhaps we should ignore the experts and follow the straightforward advice on these wonderfully naughty designs and indulge our love of food and drink without those all-too-familiar pangs of guilt.

There are six coordinated designs stitched in the yummiest candy colours and adorned with tempting cupcakes dotted with silver beads. The projects include a neat pinny to protect your clothes from give-away chocolate smudges and a stitched patch for a piggy bank to remind you of your saving priorities. For an extra sweet finishing touch you can also replace areas of the stitching with real ribbon bows.

This handy fridge magnet will remind all determined foodies that a diet need only last one day.

The sage advice on this handy apron and the other fun designs in this chapter are bound to raise a smile. Think of it this way: you are not a glutton but an explorer of food!

Apron

This design is really quick and easy to stitch and is perfect for adorning a ready-made apron, as you can see by the picture on the previous page. It also allows you to have some fun and add a real ribbon bow.

STITCH COUNT
90h x 76w
DESIGN SIZE
16.3 x 13.8cm (6½ x 5½in)
MATERIALS
* Ivory 14-count Aida 27 x 24cm
  (10½ x 9½in)
* Tapestry needle size 24
* DMC stranded cotton (floss) as listed
  in chart key
* Round silver beads 3mm diameter
* Pale blue ribbon 3mm (⅛in) wide
  x 20cm (8in) long (optional)
* Medium-weight iron-on interfacing
  the same size as the Aida
* Ready-made apron

1 Prepare for work (see page 98). Mark the centre of the fabric and centre of the chart on page 66. Use an embroidery frame if you wish.

2 Start stitching from the centre of the chart and fabric, using two strands of stranded cotton (floss) for full and three-quarter cross stitch and pink backstitch. Use one strand for dark grey backstitch. Using matching thread, attach the beads where shown on the chart. If you want to replace the cross stitched bow with a real ribbon bow refer to the box below.

3 Once all stitching is complete, make up into a patch following the instructions on page 101, but turn back the edges to leave two squares of unstitched Aida around the stitched design before sewing around the edge. Pin and tack (baste) the patch into place on the apron bib and sew around all four sides.

Ribbon Bows
If you choose to use real ribbon rather than cross stitching, make a bow as follows. Using a large-eyed needle, thread the ribbon from the front of one side of the cake, to the back and out to the front on the other side. Tie the ribbon in a bow and secure with a few stitches through the centre. Trim the ends of the ribbon neatly to finish.

Biscuit Tin

This design can be used to decorate different items, for example, a cookie jar or even a box of luxury chocolates.

STITCH COUNT
62h x 64w
DESIGN SIZE
11.3 x 11.6cm (4½ x 4⅝in)
MATERIALS
* Ivory 14-count Aida 20.3 x 20.3cm (8 x 8in)
* Tapestry needle size 24
* DMC stranded cotton (floss) as listed in chart key
* Round silver beads 3mm diameter
* Pink ribbon 3mm (⅛in) wide x 40cm (16in) long (optional)
* Medium-weight iron-on interfacing the same size as the Aida
* Biscuit tin with sides at least 13.3cm (5¼in) high
* Double-sided adhesive tape

1 Prepare for work (see page 98). Mark the centre of the fabric and centre of the chart on page 68. Use an embroidery frame if you wish.

2 Start stitching from the centre of the chart and fabric, using two strands of stranded cotton (floss) for full and three-quarter cross stitch and pink backstitch. Use one strand for dark grey backstitch. Using matching thread, attach the beads where shown on the chart. If you want to replace the cross stitched bows with real ribbon bows refer to the box opposite.

3 Once all stitching is complete, make up into a patch as described on page 101. Cover the back of the patch with strips of double-sided tape. Peel off the tape backing and stick the patch to the side of your tin.

Wine Label

This wine label shown on page 59 is very quick to stitch and because it is fastened with hook and loop tape it is easy to remove for laundering.

STITCH COUNT
52h x 46w
DESIGN SIZE
10.2 x 9cm (4 x 3½in)
MATERIALS
* Aida band in antique white with scalloped edge (54 stitches wide) 35.5cm (14in) long x 10cm (4in) wide
* Tapestry needle size 24
* DMC stranded cotton (floss) as listed in chart key
* Round 3mm silver beads
* Hook-and-loop tape (Velcro) 9cm (3½in) long

1 Prepare for work (see page 98). Mark the centre of the fabric and centre of the chart on page 67.

2 Start stitching from the centre of the chart and fabric, using two strands of stranded cotton (floss) for full and three-quarter cross stitch and pink backstitch. Use one strand for dark grey backstitch. Using matching thread, attach the beads where shown on the chart.

3 Once all stitching is complete, make up into a bottle label as follows. Trim the Aida band to 31cm (12¼in), making sure the stitched design is central. Neaten the raw edges with zigzag stitch, turn 1.3cm (½in) to the wrong side and tack (baste) down. Pin and tack one half of the Velcro tape to the wrong side of the Aida band against a short edge, and the other side of the tape on to the right side against the other short end. Sew into place around all four sides and fasten the label around the bottle.

Piggy Bank

STITCH COUNT
44h x 59w
DESIGN SIZE
8 x 10.7cm (3⅛ x 4¼in)

Start a chocolate fund with this delightful piggy bank. You will need a piggy at least 14cm (5½in) high. Use the chart on page 68 and stitch the design on an 18 x 20cm (7 x 8in) piece of ivory 14-count Aida. Use two strands of thread for full and three-quarter cross stitch. Use one strand for grey backstitch and two strands for pink. Sew on the silver beads where shown on the chart. Make the design up into a patch (see page 101). Cover the back of the patch with double-sided tape and stick to your piggy bank.

Fridge Magnet

Your one-day diet will be over by the time you stitch this naughty little project. You can change the colour of the card mount if desired.

STITCH COUNT
64h x 64w
DESIGN SIZE
11.5 x 11.5cm (4½ x 4½in)
MATERIALS
*   Ivory 14-count Aida 20.3 x 20.3cm (8 x 8in)
*   Tapestry needle size 24
*   DMC stranded cotton (floss) as listed in chart key
*   Double-fold card with square aperture of 10cm (4in) or 11.5cm (4½in)
*   Round 3mm silver beads
*   Self-adhesive magnetic strip or fridge magnet

1   Prepare for work (see page 98). Mark the centre of the fabric and centre of the chart on page 67. Use an embroidery frame if you wish.

2   Start stitching from the centre of the chart and fabric, using two strands of stranded cotton (floss) for full and three-quarter cross stitch and pink backstitch. Use one strand for dark grey backstitch. Using matching thread, attach the beads where shown on the chart.

3   Once all stitching is complete, make up into a card (see page 101), cutting a small amount from around the aperture if necessary so that all of the stitched design can be seen. Cut off the back or right-hand section of the card. Peel the tape off the magnet, stick it on to the back of the card and place the magnet on the fridge.

Shopping Bag

This useful bag is very easy to make and provides a cautionary warning for food fanatics let loose at the market.

STITCH COUNT
76h x 76w

DESIGN SIZE
13.8 x 13.8cm (5½ x 5½in)

MATERIALS
* Ivory 14-count Aida 24 x 24cm (9½ x 9½in)
* Tapestry needle size 24
* DMC stranded cotton (floss) as listed in chart key
* Round 3mm silver beads
* Pink ribbon 3mm (⅛in) wide x 20cm (8in) long (optional)
* Medium-weight iron-on interfacing the same size as the Aida
* Two pieces of fabric for the bag 46.5 x 39cm (18¼ x 15¼in)
* Webbing 2.5cm (1in) wide x 72cm (28in) long for handle

1 Prepare for work (see page 98). Mark the centre of the fabric and centre of the chart on page 69. Use an embroidery frame if you wish.

2 Start stitching from the centre of the chart and fabric, using two strands of stranded cotton (floss) for full and three-quarter cross stitch and pink backstitch. Use one strand for dark grey backstitch. Using matching thread, attach the beads where shown on the chart. To replace the cross stitched bow with a real ribbon bow see the box on page 60.

3 Once all stitching is complete, make up into a patch following the instructions on page 101, but turn back the edges to leave two Aida squares around the design before sewing around the edge.

4 Make a bag as follows. On the top edge of both pieces of bag fabric, turn 2cm (¾in) to the wrong side, press, then turn under another 2cm (¾in). Press and tack (baste) into place. Cut two pieces of webbing 36cm (14in) long for the handles. Pin and tack each end of the webbing on to the wrong side of the top edge of each bag piece 16cm (6¼in) in from the side edges. Secure the turning and the handles by topstitching 1.5cm (⅝in) down from the top edge.

5 Measure 9cm (3½in) down from the top and place a pin, then measure across the width and mark the centre. Place the top of the patch against these markers, making sure that the centre of the patch matches the centre of the bag width. Pin and tack (baste) the patch into place, making sure it is straight. Sew the patch on to the bag piece around all sides.

6 With right sides facing, stitch the two bag pieces together around three sides, leaving the top edge open. Neaten the seam allowance. Turn the bag through to the right side and press to finish.

Indulge yourself by all means but do remember, it's never a good idea to eat more than you can lift!

Apron

DMC stranded cotton
Cross stitch

- 208
- 211
- 369
- 605
- × 745
- 3761
- 3820
- 3822
- blanc

Backstitch

— 414 (1 strand)
— 3607 (2 strands)

Round beads

silver

The stitched ribbon on the
cake can be replaced with
real ribbon and a bow –
see page 60 for instructions

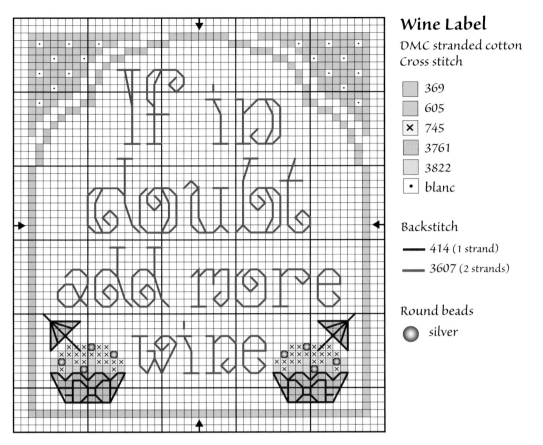

Wine Label

DMC stranded cotton
Cross stitch

▨	369
▨	605
✕	745
▨	3761
▨	3822
•	blanc

Backstitch

―― 414 (1 strand)
―― 3607 (2 strands)

Round beads

⬤ silver

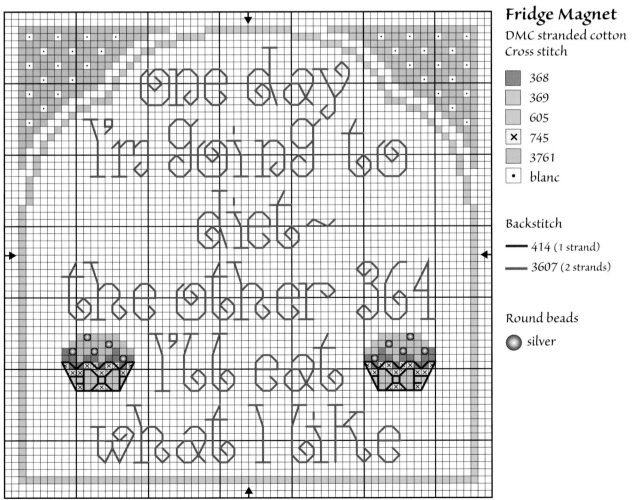

Fridge Magnet

DMC stranded cotton
Cross stitch

▨	368
▨	369
▨	605
✕	745
▨	3761
•	blanc

Backstitch

―― 414 (1 strand)
―― 3607 (2 strands)

Round beads

⬤ silver

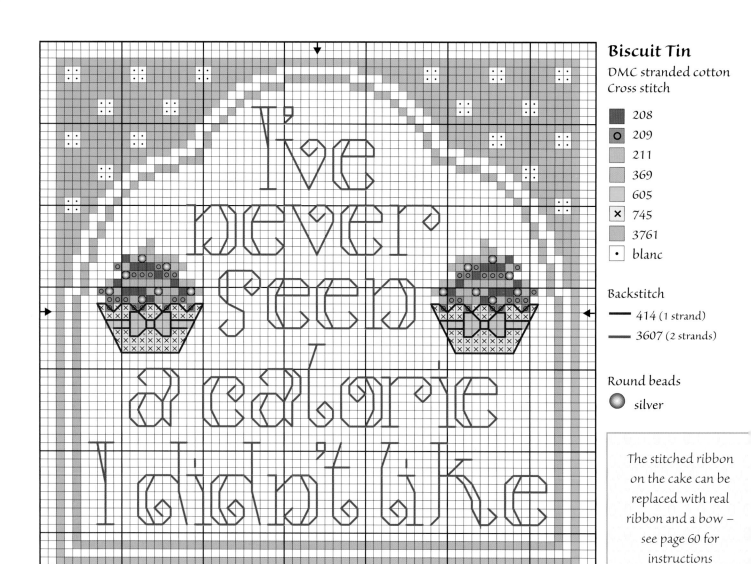

Biscuit Tin

DMC stranded cotton
Cross stitch

■	208
⊙	209
	211
	369
	605
✕	745
	3761
•	blanc

Backstitch

— 414 (1 strand)
— 3607 (2 strands)

Round beads

⬤ silver

The stitched ribbon
on the cake can be
replaced with real
ribbon and a bow –
see page 60 for
instructions

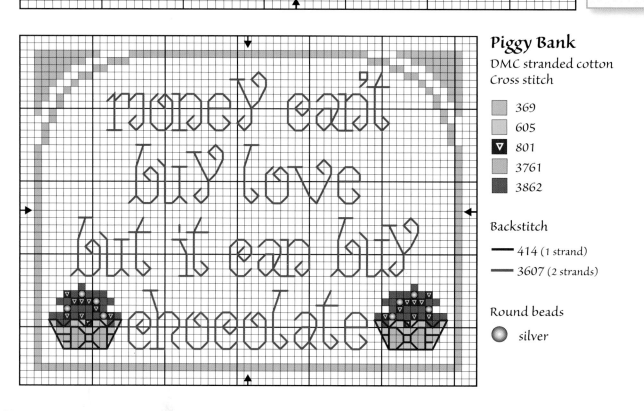

Piggy Bank

DMC stranded cotton
Cross stitch

	369
	605
▽	801
	3761
	3862

Backstitch

— 414 (1 strand)
— 3607 (2 strands)

Round beads

⬤ silver

Shopping Bag

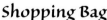
DMC stranded cotton
Cross stitch

▨ 211	▨ 605	▨ 3822
▨ 368	✕ 745	• blanc
▨ 369	▨ 3761	

Backstitch

— 414 (1 strand)

— 3607 (2 strands)

Round beads

⬤ silver

The stitched ribbon on the cake can be replaced with real ribbon and a bow – see page 60 for instructions

Men are from Mars...

There's a place for love and romance in every girl's life, whatever her age, but make sure the man in your life knows it's on *your* terms. There are five love-themed projects in this chapter that will make ideal gifts for Valentine's Day and wedding anniversaries (if you get that far). They will also remind him who's really in control in the relationship.

The tongue-in-cheek sentiments, whether on a Valentine's card with a material-girl statement or a teddy perfect for post-fight making up, make it clear that although your man thinks he's the boss, you are the decision maker. Traditional romantic symbols of hearts, flowers and butterflies take the sting out of the messages – almost. And anyway, who wants to be saccharine sweet when you can keep him guessing with smart and sassy?

Hang this teasing sign in your car or at your desk to show the world how much you really care about the man in your life.

A cuddly cat seems like a fair trade if he turns out not to be 'the one'; and if he is then a sampler will remind you that marriage is the only war where you sleep with the enemy.

This tongue-in-cheek sentiment made up as a picture (see previous page) could be stitched on finer 18-count fabric to create a smaller finished design size, perhaps for a card.

STITCH COUNT
110h x 83w

DESIGN SIZE
20 x 15cm (7⅞ x 6in)

MATERIALS
* Antique white 14-count Aida 30.5 x 24cm (12 x 9½in)
* Tapestry needle size 24
* DMC stranded cotton (floss) as listed in chart key
* Frame to fit the embroidery
* Mount board
* Thin wadding (batting)
* Double-sided adhesive tape

1 Prepare for work (see page 98). Mark the centre of the fabric and centre of the chart on page 75. Use an embroidery frame if you wish.

2 Start stitching from the centre of the chart and fabric, using two strands of stranded cotton (floss) for full and three-quarter cross stitches. Use one strand for mauve backstitches and two strands for dark purple backstitches.

3 Once all stitching is complete, finish your picture by mounting and framing (see page 102).

Love Heart Pillow

This pillow design would also make a unique gift tag or card. Follow steps 1 and 2 above to stitch the design using the chart on page 76. Stitch on a 15.2cm (6in) square of 14-count antique white Aida. Make up into a heart-shaped sign as described in step 3 on page 43. Fold a piece of ribbon 6mm (¼in) wide x 60cm (24in) long in half, stitch in the middle of the top edge and tie into a knot. Leave a hanging loop of about 8cm (3¼in) and tie the ends into a bow, tying the loops once more so that the bow doesn't undo.

STITCH COUNT
55h x 55w

DESIGN SIZE
10 x 10cm (4 x 4in)

This amusing label (see also the picture on page 71) could also be stitched and made up as a fridge magnet or a coaster. The word 'Husband' can be replaced with 'Boyfriend' or 'Man' as charted on page 77.

STITCH COUNT
32h x 45w
DESIGN SIZE
5.8 x 8.2cm (2¼ x 3¼in)
MATERIALS
* Antique white 14-count Aida 11 x 13.5cm (4¼ x 5¼in)
* Tapestry needle size 24
* DMC stranded cotton (floss) as listed in chart key
* Backing fabric the same size as the Aida
* Medium-weight iron-on interfacing same size as the Aida
* Ribbon 6mm (¼in) wide x 60cm (24in) long
* Cat soft toy

1 Prepare for work (see page 98). Mark the centre of the fabric and centre of the chart on page 77. Use an embroidery frame if you wish.

2 Start stitching from the centre of the chart and fabric, using two strands of stranded cotton (floss) for full and three-quarter cross stitches. Use one strand for mauve backstitches and two strands for dark purple. Personalize your label by using the alternative words from the chart on page 77.

3 Once all stitching is complete, make up into a label as follows. Fuse the iron-on interfacing to the wrong side of the embroidery according to the manufacturer's instructions.

4 With right sides facing, place the embroidery on to the backing fabric. Stitching one square of Aida away from the embroidery, sew around three sides, leaving one short side open. Trim the seam allowance to 1cm (³/₈in), including along the open edge. Turn through to the right side, press and sew the open edge closed.

5 Fold the ribbon in half and stitch in the middle of the top edge on the wrong side. Tie into a bow, tying the loops once more so that the bow doesn't undo. Place around the neck of the soft toy and tie the ends. Trim the excess ribbon to finish.

Valentine Card

Send this cheeky invitation to your special someone on Valentine's Day.

STITCH COUNT
51h x 51w
DESIGN SIZE
9.3 x 9.3cm (3¾ x 3¾in)
MATERIALS
* Antique white 14-count Aida
  15.2 x 15.2cm (6 x 6in)
* Tapestry needle size 24
* DMC stranded cotton (floss) as listed in
  chart key
* Double-fold card with 10cm (4in)
  square aperture
* Heart embellishments

1 Prepare for work (see page 98). Mark the centre of the fabric and centre of the chart on page 77.

2 Start stitching from the centre of the chart and fabric, using two strands of stranded cotton (floss) for full and three-quarter cross stitches. Use one strand for mauve backstitches and two strands for dark purple backstitches.

3 Once all stitching is complete, make up into a card (see page 101). Finish by sticking the heart embellishments on to the card.

Bear Heart

Stitch up this sign to give with a cute teddy gift. For this slightly smaller heart, use the chart on page 76 and stitch on a 15.2cm (6in) square of 14-count antique white Aida, using two strands for cross stitch. Use one strand for mauve backstitches and two strands for dark purple. Back with interfacing as described on page 101 but omit the hanging ribbon and sew the heart to the bear's paws.

STITCH COUNT
47h x 49w
DESIGN SIZE
8.5 x 9cm (3³⁄₈ x 3½in)

Mr Right Picture

DMC stranded cotton

Cross stitch

■	917	✗	3607	▨	3609

Backstitch

— 208 (1 strand)　　　— 550 (2 strands)

Bear Heart and Love Heart Pillow

DMC stranded cotton
Cross stitch

■	917
⊠	3607
▨	3609

Backstitch

——	208 (1 strand)
——	550 (2 strands)

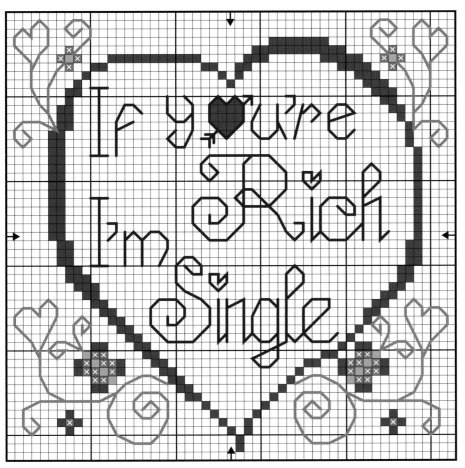

DMC stranded cotton
Cross stitch

■	917
⊠	3607
▨	3609

Backstitch

——	208 (1 strand)
——	550 (2 strands)

You can replace the
word Husband with
either of the words
charted here

Family Fun

The saying goes that you can choose your friends but not your relatives, and oh how true that is. However, as the Burmese proverb reminds us, in time of test, family is best. So when the antics of your nearest and dearest are driving you to distraction, keep a sense of perspective and get even by displaying some of their idiosyncrasies in cross stitch for the whole world to see!

The five pictures in this chapter are wry snapshots of family life and have a charming folk-art look, brought up to date with contemporary framing. They have also been embellished with gingham ribbons and buttons, although the motifs could be cross stitched instead.

Children are a great comfort in your old age – but may help you reach it faster! Remind yourself of their 'delights' with the Homemade Gifts Sampler shown overleaf and detailed here.

These four pictures celebrate family life and remind us that families are a bit like fudge – mostly sweet but there's bound to be a few nuts.

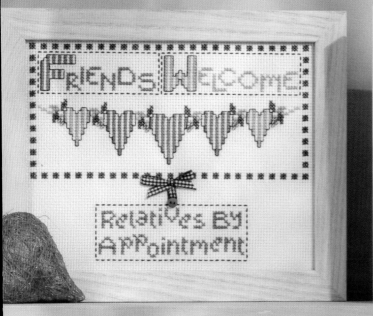

FRiENDS WeLCOME

Relatives By
AppoiNtment

OUr
FAMiLY
TRee
is full
of nuts

INSANity
Is
HEReDiTARY
You get it from
your kids

Sisters &
Chocolate
make life
bearable

(not necessarily in that order)

Homemade Gifts Sampler

This wry look at the joys of children could be personalized for your family by stitching more or less children; to add more simply extend the side borders and repeat some of the child figures, perhaps changing the hair colours. This design also uses some attractive embellishments – see the tinted box below.

STITCH COUNT
98h x 126w
DESIGN SIZE
17.8 x 23 x (7 x 9in)
MATERIALS
* Ivory 14-count Aida 33 x 38cm (13 x 15in)
* Tapestry needle size 24
* DMC stranded cotton (floss) as listed in chart key
* Three heart buttons 1.3cm (½in) wide and two round buttons 6mm (¼in) diameter (optional)
* Green gingham ribbon 6mm (¼in) wide x 40cm (16in) long (optional)
* Frame to fit the embroidery
* Mount board
* Thin wadding (batting)
* Double-sided adhesive tape

1 Prepare for work (see page 98). Mark the centre of the fabric and centre of the chart on pages 84–85. Use an embroidery frame if you wish.

2 Start stitching from the centre of the chart and fabric, using two strands of stranded cotton (floss) for cross stitches and for backstitches.

3 If you want to add the button and bows embellishments, refer to the box below. Once all stitching is complete, finish your picture by mounting and framing (see page 102).

Buttons and Bows
Instead of stitching the small hearts, you could sew on three heart-shaped buttons in colours to match the design.

The stitched bows on the large hearts can also be replaced with real ribbon bows as follows. Cut two 20cm (8in) lengths of ribbon. Fold one ribbon in half, place the fold to the top of one of the hearts and sew in place along the fold. Lay the two ends of the ribbon up to just under the top border and sew in place. Tie the ends in a bow and secure with a few stitches through the centre. Trim the ends of the ribbon. Sew a small button on to the fold of the ribbon. Repeat for the other heart.

I Love To Give
HomeMade Gifts
-Which one do You Want?

The four cheeky designs shown on page 79 will help you to keep a smile on your face on even the most trying of days. The stitching instructions are similar for all four designs and the embellishments are optional. Refer to the charts for the stitch counts and design sizes.

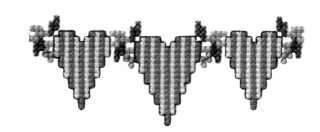

1   Prepare for work (see page 98) and stitch from the centre of the chart and fabric. Use the charts on pages 86–89 and follow step 2 on page 80 for stitching the designs. Where beads are used, use two strands of thread to attach them. To add button or bow embellishments, refer to the box on page 80.

2   Once all stitching is complete, make up into a framed picture (see page 102).

MATERIALS (for each design)
* Tapestry needle size 24
* DMC stranded cotton (floss) as listed in chart key
* Frame to fit the embroidery
* Mount board
* Thin wadding (batting)
* Double-sided adhesive tape

OUR FAMILY TREE
* Ivory 14-count Aida 28.5 x 28.5cm (11¼ x 11¼in)
* Mill Hill glass seed beads 02023

INSANITY IS HEREDITARY
* Ivory 14-count Aida 28.5 x 28.5cm (11¼ x 11¼in)
* Mill Hill antique glass beads 03057

FRIENDS WELCOME
* Ivory 14-count Aida 28.5 x 33cm (11¼ x 13in)
* Mill Hill antique glass beads 03057
* Small green button 6mm (¼in) diameter
* Green gingham ribbon 6mm (¼in) wide x 20cm (8in) long (optional)

SISTERS AND CHOCOLATE
* Ivory 14-count Aida 28.5 x 33cm (11¼ x 13in)
* Two brown heart buttons 1.3cm (½in) wide and one brown round button 6mm (¼in) diameter
* Dark red gingham ribbon 6mm (¼in) wide x 20cm (8in) long (optional)

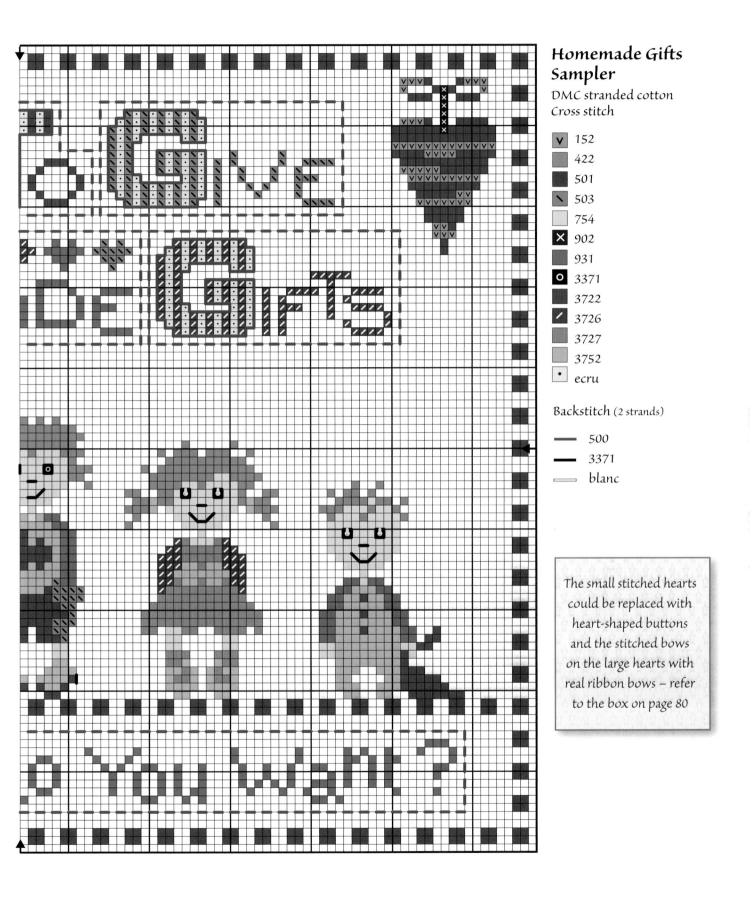

Homemade Gifts Sampler

DMC stranded cotton
Cross stitch

v	152
	422
	501
\	503
	754
✕	902
	931
⊙	3371
	3722
/	3726
	3727
	3752
•	ecru

Backstitch (2 strands)

——	500
——	3371
——	blanc

The small stitched hearts
could be replaced with
heart-shaped buttons
and the stitched bows
on the large hearts with
real ribbon bows – refer
to the box on page 80

Our Family Tree

DMC stranded cotton
Cross stitch

◥ 501	◆ 3031	⊡ ecru		
503	+ 3862			
931	3864			

Backstitch
— 500
— 3031

Mill Hill seed beads
● 02023 root beer

Stitch count
74h x 74w

Design size
13.5 x 13.5cm
(5¼ x 5¼in)

Insanity is Hereditary

DMC stranded cotton
Cross stitch

	Backstitch	Mill Hill Antique seed beads
V 152	— 500	⬤ 03057 cherry sorbet
422		
501		
503		
931		
3722		
• ecru		

Stitch count
74h x 74w
Design size
13.5 x 13.5cm
(5¼ x 5¼in)

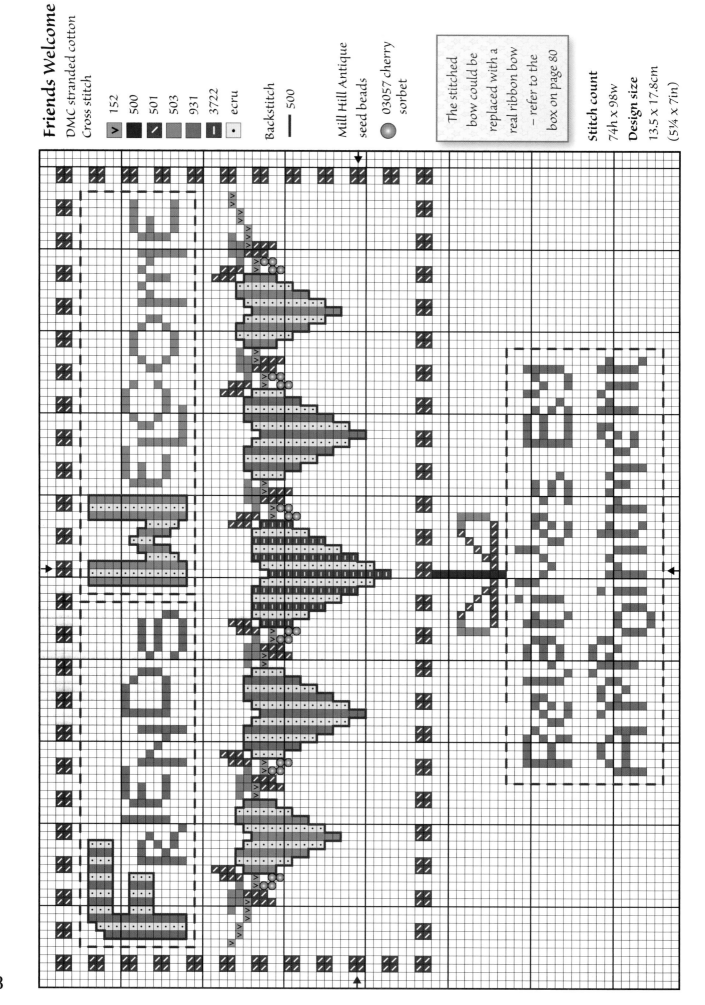

Friends Welcome

DMC stranded cotton
Cross stitch

- V 152
- ■ 500
- ⁄ 501
- ▨ 503
- ▨ 931
- I 3722
- · ecru

Backstitch
— 500

Mill Hill Antique seed beads
● 03057 cherry sorbet

The stitched bow could be replaced with a real ribbon bow – refer to the box on page 80

Stitch count
74h x 98w
Design size
13.5 x 17.8cm
(5¼ x 7in)

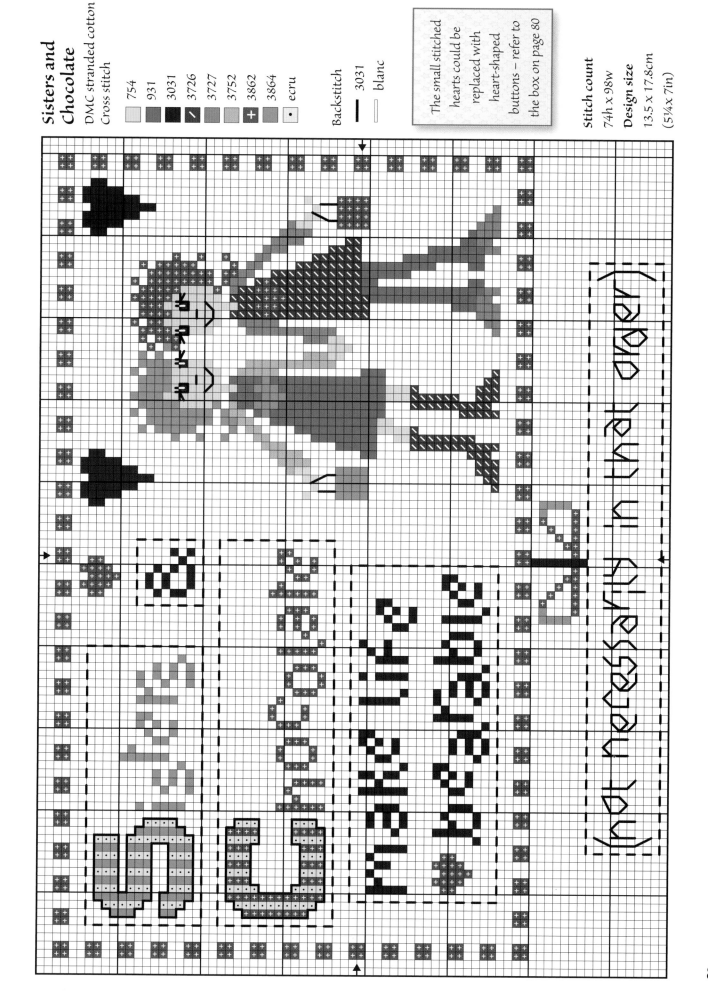

Sisters and Chocolate

DMC stranded cotton
Cross stitch

	754
	931
	3031
/	3726
	3727
	3752
+	3862
	3864
·	ecru

Backstitch

▬	3031
▭	blanc

The small stitched hearts could be replaced with heart-shaped buttons – refer to the box on page 80

Stitch count
74h x 98w
Design size
13.5 x 17.8cm
(5¼ x 7in)

Saving the Planet

After being nagged to recycle, reduce and re-use everything, you can hardly be blamed for staging a small rebellion. Yes, you know about limiting global warming and the need to save water and reduce carbon emissions, but does is it all have to be doom and gloom? Having a sense of humour will make saving the planet a lot more fun!

These four designs add a naughty twist to familiar messages. For the chocoholic and wine connoisseur, a hanging pillow sign and bottle bag give more important reasons for being eco-friendly. A cute car buddy encourages you to get your priorities in the right order as you go green, and it'll be easier to say no to plastic bags with a fashionable tote bag.

This little pillow sign is really easy to make and can be hung in your car, at work or at home.

On a visit to the shops one bag is never enough, so take along this stylish tote bag and a useful bottle bag (see page 93) and reduce the need for plastic alternatives.

Tote Bag

This tote bag should last for a long time if you use a sturdy fabric such as denim or canvas. Alternatively, you could attach the embroidered patch to a ready-made bag.

STITCH COUNT
66h x 101w
DESIGN SIZE
12 x 18.3cm (4¾ x 7¼in)
MATERIALS
* White 14-count Aida 23 x 28cm (9 x 11in)
* Tapestry needle size 24
* DMC stranded cotton (floss) as listed in chart key
* Piece of medium-weight iron-on interfacing the same size as Aida
* Two pieces of fabric for bag 46.5 x 39cm (18¼ x 15¼in)
* Webbing tape 2.5cm (1in) wide x 72cm (28in) long

1 Prepare for work (see page 98). Mark the centre of the fabric and centre of the chart on page 96. Use an embroidery frame if you wish.

2 Start stitching from the centre of the chart and fabric, using two strands of stranded cotton (floss) for cross stitch, backstitch and French knots. Once all stitching is complete, make up into a patch following step 3 for the make-up bag on page 12.

3 Make a bag and sew on the patch following steps 4–6 for the shopping bag on page 64.

Planet Pillow Sign

This little pillow sign would be a great gift for a chocoholic friend. Use the chart on page 97 and stitch the design on a 23 x 25.5cm (9 x 10in) piece of white 14-count Aida. Use two strands of thread for cross stitch, backstitch and French knots. Using a piece of backing fabric the same size as the Aida, make up into a pillow sign following steps 3–5 on page 21 using a 23cm (9in) length of braid or piping cord for a handle.

STITCH COUNT
66h x 85w
DESIGN SIZE
12 x 15.2cm (4¾ x 6in)

Bottle Bag

This bottle bag can be used for any container of liquid – alcoholic or otherwise! Using a strong fabric such as denim or canvas creates a hard-wearing bag, while wide webbing tape is ideal for strong handles.

STITCH COUNT
61h x 68w

DESIGN SIZE
11 x 12.3cm (4³/₈ x 4⁷/₈in)

MATERIALS
* White 14-count Aida 23 x 23cm (9 x 9in)
* Tapestry needle size 24
* DMC stranded cotton (floss) as listed in chart key
* Piece of medium-weight iron-on interfacing same size as Aida
* Two pieces of strong fabric for bag 36 x 36cm (14 x 14in)
* Webbing tape 2.5cm (1in) x 72cm (28in) long

1 Prepare for work (see page 98). Mark the centre of the bag fabric and centre of the chart on page 95. Use an embroidery frame if you wish.

2 Start stitching from the centre of the chart and fabric, using two strands of stranded cotton (floss) for cross stitch, backstitch and French knots. Once all stitching is complete, make up into a patch following step 3 for the make-up bag on page 12.

3 To position the patch, on the right side of one piece of bag fabric, measure 3cm (1¼in) in from the left edge and place a pin. Measure 8cm (3¼in) down from top edge and place a pin. Line the patch up with these markers and pin and tack (baste) in place. Sew around all four sides.

4 Make the bag as follows. Turn 1cm (³/₈in) to the wrong side along the top edge of each bag piece and press. Turn over another 1cm (³/₈in) and press. Tack (baste) the turning in place. Cut the webbing in half to make two handles 36cm (14in) long and pin each handle in place on the wrong side of the top edge 11cm (4¼in) in from each side. Tack in place. Secure the turning and the handles by topstitching 1.3cm (½in) down from the top edge.

5 With right sides facing, stitch the two bag pieces together around three sides, leaving the top open. Neaten the seam allowance. Turn the bag through to the right side and press. To divide into two pockets, fold the bag in half vertically and press the fold. Unfold the bag and stitch a line down this fold through all thicknesses.

Car Buddy

This car buddy may help you remember eco-friendly advice when driving, or it may just make you and your passengers smile.

STITCH COUNT
58h x 58
DESIGN SIZE
9.2 x 9.2cm (3¾ x 3¾in)
MATERIALS
* White 16-count Aida 19 x 19cm
  (7½ x 7½in)
* Tapestry needle size 24
* DMC stranded cotton (floss) as listed
  in chart key
* Two pieces of felt 30.5 x 25.5cm
  (12 x 10in)
* Tracing paper
* Polyester toy stuffing
* Buttons, two white and one black
* Narrow ribbon 23cm (9in) long

1 Prepare for work (see page 98). Mark the centre of the fabric and centre of the chart opposite. Use an embroidery frame if you wish.

2 Start stitching from the centre of the chart and fabric, using two strands of stranded cotton (floss) for cross stitch, backstitch and French knots. Once all stitching is complete, make up into a patch following step 3 for the make-up bag on page 12.

3 Make a car buddy and sew on the patch following steps 3–5 for the computer buddy on page 20. Sew on buttons in place of embroidered eyes. Fold the ribbon in half and sew on to the back between the ears as a hanging loop.

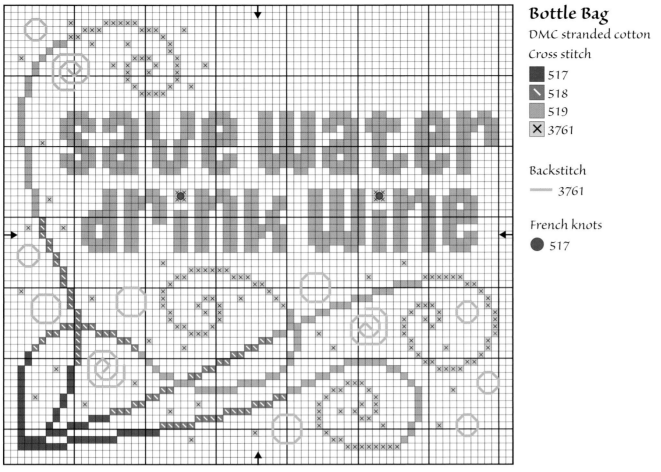

Bottle Bag

DMC stranded cotton

Cross stitch

- ■ 517
- ＼ 518
- ■ 519
- ✕ 3761

Backstitch

— 3761

French knots

● 517

Car Buddy

DMC stranded cotton

Cross stitch

- ■ 319
- ＋ 367
- ■ 368
- — 369
- ▪ 564

Backstitch

— 319
— 564

French knots

● 562

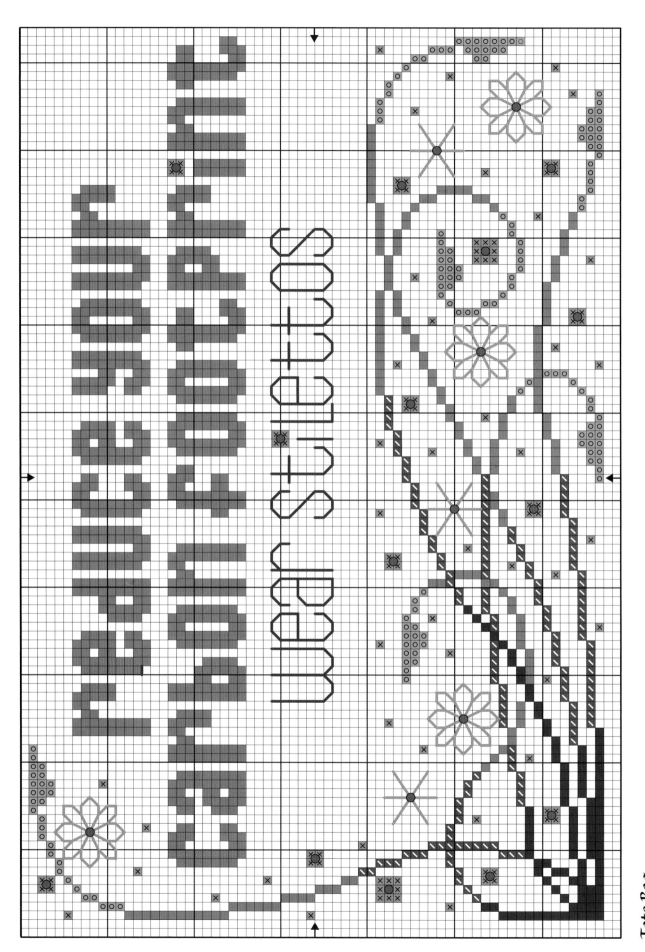

Tote Bag

DMC stranded cotton

Cross stitch

316   962   3726   3802   962   3727

Backstitch
— 962
— 3802

French knots
● 3687

Planet Pillow Sign

DMC stranded cotton

Cross stitch

/	839
▪	3031
◉	3859
■	3863
∨	3864

Backsstitch

——— 3031
——— 3859

French knots
● 3858

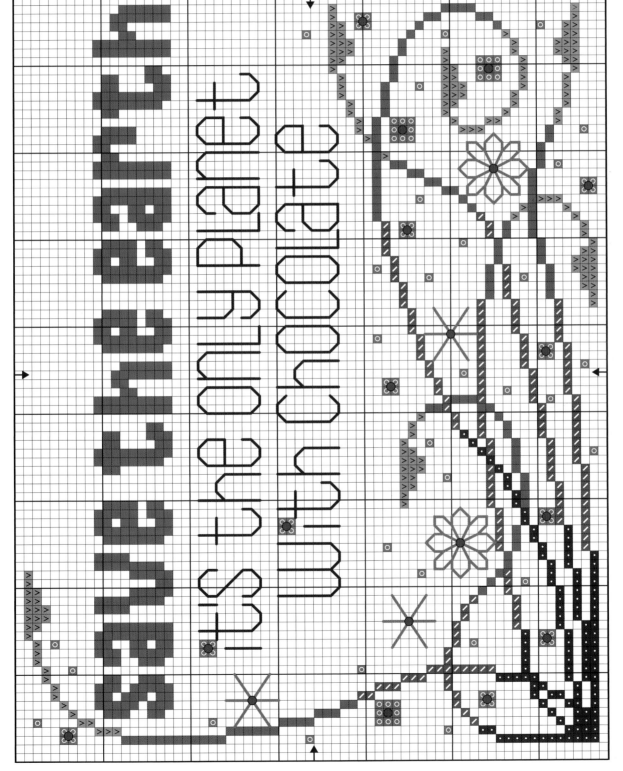

Materials and Techniques

This section will be very useful to beginners as it describes the materials and equipment required for cross stitch and the basic stitching techniques used.

Materials

Fabric

The designs have been worked on Aida fabric, where one block corresponds to one square on the chart and one cross stitch is made over one block using the holes as a guide. The designs could also be stitched on a 28-count evenweave such as linen but you will need to work over two fabric threads. A design worked on 14-count Aida will be the same size if stitched over two threads on 28-count evenweave.

Fabric Size

If you want to frame your design, add at least 10cm (4in) to both measurements of the finished design size. This will give you plenty of fabric to stretch and mount on to a board. If the design is going into card, add at least 5cm (2in) to the measurements of the aperture to allow for making up. If making into a patch, add at least 5cm (2in) to allow for turnings.

Threads

The projects have been stitched with DMC stranded embroidery cotton (floss) but you could match the colours to other thread ranges – ask at your local needlework store. Some Light Effects metallic threads have also been used. These threads are in six-stranded skeins, which can be split into separate strands. The project instructions tell you how many strands to use.

Tweeded cross stitch means combining two threads in the needle at the same time and working as one to create a mottled effect. The two colours will be listed together in the key. For example, blanc + E5200 means using one strand of blanc together with one strand of E5200.

Needles

Tapestry needles are used for cross stitch as they have a round point, usually sizes 24–26. If the design uses three-quarter cross stitches, have a sharp needle handy to pierce a hole in the centre of the Aida square. A thinner beading needle will be needed to sew on seed beads.

Frames

It is a matter of personal preference as to whether you use an embroidery frame to keep your fabric taut while stitching. Generally speaking, working with a frame helps to keep the tension even and prevent distortion, while working without a frame is faster and less cumbersome. There are various types on the market – look in your local needlework store for some examples.

Techniques

Preparing to Stitch

Before starting work, check the design size given with each project and make sure that this is the size you require for your finished embroidery. Your fabric should be 5–10cm (2–4in) larger all the way round than the finished size of the stitching, to allow for making up. Cut your fabric to size. To prevent fraying, machine around the edges with a zigzag stitch. To find the centre, fold the fabric in half and then half again. Place a pin or a small tacking (basting) stitch where the two folds cross. Press the fabric flat. Place a mark at the centre of the chart. Begin stitching from the middle of the fabric and the middle of the chart and this will ensure that the finished design is centred on the fabric.

Calculating Design Size

Each project gives the stitch count and finished design size but if you plan to work the design on a different count fabric and want to check the size of fabric needed, you will need to be able to calculate the finished size. Work out the finished size of any design by dividing the number of stitches in the height and the number of stitches in the width by the fabric count. For example, a design with a stitch count of 28h x 42w when stitched on 14-count Aida would have a finished size of 2 x 3in: $28 \div 14 = 2in$ and $42 \div 14 = 3in$. So you would need a piece of fabric 2 x 3in (5 x 7.5cm) plus extra for making up.

When using aperture cards or ready-made items, measure the aperture or size of the item and compare it with the design size of your chosen motif. If it is too big to fit when worked on 14-count fabric, it may fit if worked on 16-count as the finished size will be smaller. Always allow a small margin of fabric between the motif and the aperture so that the motif doesn't look as if it has been forced into the space. When working on Aida bands, count the number of stitches on the band width to make sure your design will fit.

Using Charts and Keys

The charts in this book are in colour with some colours further identified with black or white symbols.

* Each coloured square on the chart represents one cross stitch and each empty square represents unworked fabric. On Aida fabric this is one block and on evenweave it is two threads.
* Each complete chart has arrows at the side to show the centre point, which you could mark with a pen.
* Some designs use three-quarter cross stitches, sometimes called fractional stitches. These are represented by a coloured triangle instead of a full coloured square.
* Each chart has a key, which tells you what colours and codes to use.
* Backstitch is shown by a coloured line on the chart, with the code given in the key.
* French knots are shown by coloured circles, with the code given in the key.
* Seed beads are indicated by larger coloured circles.

Washing and Pressing

If stitching requires washing, hand wash gently in warm water with a non-biological washing powder or liquid. Roll the stitching in a towel to blot off most of the water – never wring your stitching or you will distort the stitches. Cover your ironing board with a towel to prevent flattening the stitches, and press the stitching on the wrong side until dry.

The Stitches

Starting and Finishing Stitching

Avoid using knots when starting and finishing as this will make your work uneven and lumpy when mounted. Instead, bring the needle up at the start of the first stitch, leaving a 'tail' of about 2.5cm (1in) at the back. Secure this tail by working the first few stitches over it. Start new threads by first passing the needle through several stitches on the back of the work.

To finish off thread, pass the needle through several nearby stitches on the wrong side of the work, then cut the thread off, close to the fabric.

Cross Stitch

A cross stitch can be worked singly (Fig 1a) or half stitches can be sewn in a line and completed on the return journey (Fig 1b). A half cross stitch is simply a single diagonal line.

To make a full cross stitch over one block of Aida, bring the needle up through the fabric at the bottom left side of the stitch (number 1 on Fig 1a) and cross diagonally to the top right corner (2). Push the needle through the hole and bring up through at 3, crossing the fabric diagonally to finish the stitch at 4. To work the next stitch, come up through the bottom right corner of the first stitch and repeat the sequence.

To work a line of cross stitches, stitch the first part of the stitch as before and repeat these half cross stitches along the row. Complete the crosses on the way back. Note: for neat work, always finish the cross stitches with the top stitches lying in the same diagonal direction.

Fig 1b Working cross stitch in two journeys

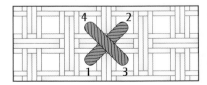

Fig 1a Working a single cross stitch

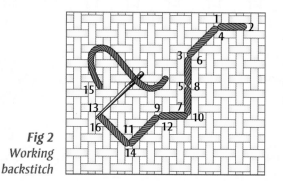

Backstitch

Backstitches are used to give definition to parts of a design and to outline areas. Many of the charts use different coloured backstitches. Follow Fig 2, bringing the needle up at 1, down at 2, up again at 3, down at 4 and so on.

Fig 2
Working
backstitch

Three-quarter Cross Stitch

Three-quarter cross stitches give more detail to a design and can create the illusion of curves. They are shown by a triangle within a square on the charts. These stitches are easier on evenweave fabric than Aida (see Fig 3). To work on Aida, make a half cross stitch from corner to corner and then work a quarter stitch from the other corner into the centre of the Aida square, piercing the fabric and anchoring the half stitch.

Fig 3
Working
three-
quarter
cross stitch

French Knot

French knots have been used as eye highlights and details in some of the designs in various colours.

To work, follow Fig 4, bringing the needle and thread up through the fabric at the exact place where the knot is to be positioned. Wrap the thread once or twice around the needle (according to the project instructions), holding the thread firmly close to the needle, then twist the needle back through the fabric as close as possible to where it first emerged. Holding the knot down carefully, pull the thread through to the back leaving the knot on the surface, securing it with one small stitch on the back.

Fig 4 Working a French knot

Attaching Beads

Adding beads will bring sparkle and texture to your cross stitch embroidery. Attach seed beads using ordinary sewing thread that matches the fabric colour and a beading needle or very fine 'sharp' needle. Use half cross stitch if sewing beads on in place of cross stitch.

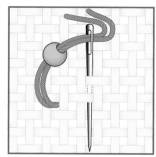
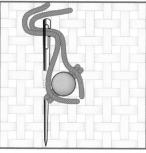

Fig 5 Attaching a bead as part of a cross stitch

Making Up

Each design is made up into a finished project with detailed making up instructions. However, your favourite design may be presented as a card when you would prefer to have it as a framed picture or make it into a pillow sign. To do this, simply stitch your chosen design and follow the making up instructions elsewhere in the book. Remember to add extra fabric if you want to frame your design (see Fabric Size, page 98).

Using Iron-on Interfacing

Many of the stitched designs have been used as patches, which makes them extremely versatile and allows you to use them to decorate all sorts of objects. The embroidery is backed with a medium weight, iron-on interfacing to prevent fraying when cutting into shape and also to add stiffness to the patch.

1 Cut a piece of interfacing the same size as the Aida. Set the iron to the manufacturer's recommended heating. Test on waste fabric and interfacing first to make sure that they will bond without scorching the design. Place the stitching face down on to a towel and iron on the interfacing.

2 Trim the patch to size and then attach to your object by stitching or use fabric glue.

Mounting Work in Cards

Many of the designs in the book make great greetings cards and there are many card blanks available from stores and online. To make your own aperture card see step 3 on page 53.

1 Once all stitching is complete, mount into a card as follows. Lay the card right side up on top of the design so the stitching is in the middle of the aperture. Place a pin at each corner of the fabric and remove the card. Trim the fabric to within about 1.3cm (½in) so it will fit inside the card when it is made up.

2 On the wrong side of the card, stick double-sided tape around the aperture and peel off the backing strip. With the stitching right side up, place the card over the design using the pins to guide it into position. Press down firmly around the aperture so the fabric is stuck securely to the card.

3 Place the card face down with the top of the design at the top. On the wrong side of the card, stick more double-sided tape around the edge of the middle section and peel off the backing tape. Fold in the left section to cover the back of the stitching and press down firmly. Fold in the right section to finish.

Framing Work

With so many ready-made frames available in all sorts of shops it is easy to display your cross stitch as a framed picture.

1 Cut a piece of mount board to fit the frame aperture (draw around the backing board from the frame). Using double-sided tape, stick a piece of wadding (batting) to the mount board and trim the wadding to the same size using a sharp craft knife.

2 Lay the embroidery right side up on to the wadding, making sure the design is central and straight, matching a fabric thread along the edges. Push pins through at the four corners and along the edges to mark the position. Trim the fabric to leave 7.5cm (3in) all around.

3 Turn the embroidery and mount board over together. Stick double-sided tape around the edges of the board to a depth of 5cm (2in) and peel off the backing. Fold the excess fabric back, pressing down firmly to stick the fabric to the board, adding more tape to neaten the corners. Remove the pins and reassemble the frame with the embroidery in it.

Tips for Perfect Stitching

Cross stitch is one of the easiest forms of counted embroidery. Following these useful pointers will help you to produce consistently neat work and save you time.

* Before starting, check the design size given with each project and make sure that this is the size you require for your finished embroidery. The fabric you are stitching on should be at least 5–10cm (2– 4in) larger all round than the finished size of the stitching, to allow for making up.

* Organize your threads before you start a project as this will help to avoid confusion later. Put the threads required for a particular project on an organizer (available from craft shops) and always include the manufacturer's name and the shade number. You can make your own thread organizer by punching holes along one side of a piece of thick card.

* When you have cut the length of stranded cotton (floss) you need, usually about 46cm (18in), separate out all the strands before taking the number you need, realigning them and threading your needle.

* If using a hoop, avoid placing it over worked stitches and remove it from the fabric at the end of a stitching session.

* For neat cross stitching, work the top stitches so they all face in the same direction.

* If your thread begins to twist, turn the work upside down and let the needle spin freely for a few seconds.

* If adding a backstitch outline, always add it after the cross stitch has been completed to prevent the solid line of the backstitch being broken.

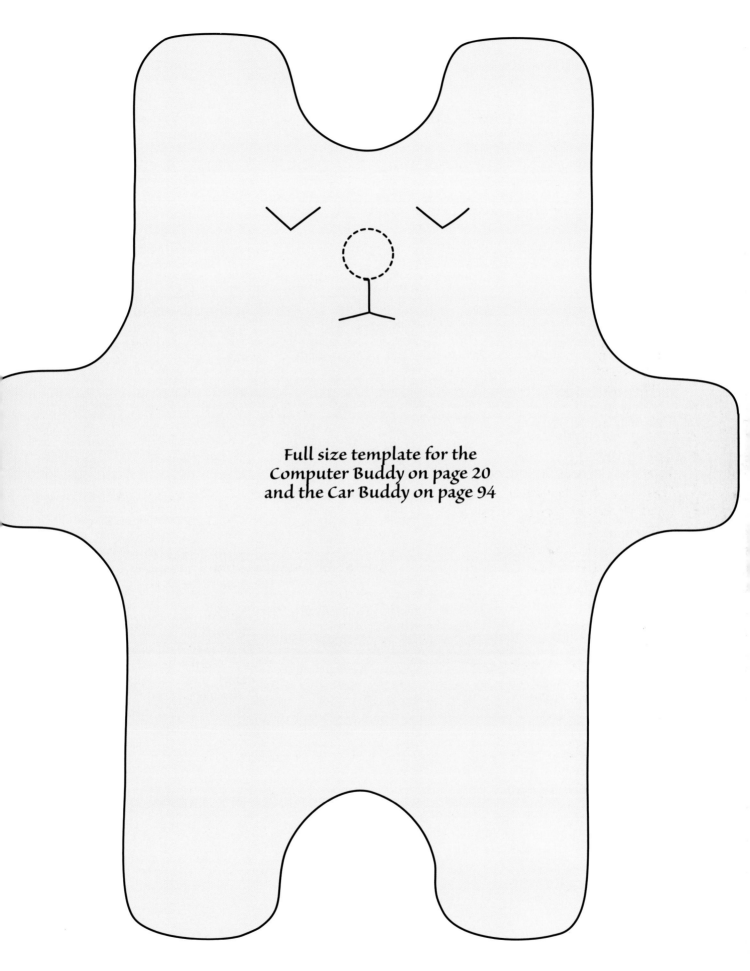

Full size template for the
Computer Buddy on page 20
and the Car Buddy on page 94

Suppliers

The following suppliers will have the materials and equipment you need to work the designs in this book. Contact the manufacturers for your local stockist or find local stockists and mail order information on their websites.

UK

Beads Unlimited
PO Box 1, Hove, BN3 3SG
Tel: 01273 740777
www.beadsunlimited.co.uk
For round silver beads

Coats Crafts UK
PO Box 22, Lingfield Estate, Mullen
Road, Darlington, County Durham,
DL1 1YQ
Tel: 01325 394237 (for stockists)
www.coatscrafts.co.uk
*For Anchor threads (Coats also stock
some Charles Craft products, for towels
with Aida inserts)*

Craft Creations Ltd
Ingersoll House, Delamare Road,
Cheshunt, Hertfordshire, EN8 9HD
Tel: 01992 781900
www.craftcreations.co.uk
For aperture cards

Crafty Bitz
22 Seymour Gardens, Ilford,
Essex, IG1 3LN
Tel: 0845 2300 969
www.craftybitz.co.uk
For card embellishments

DMC Creative World Ltd
1st Floor Compass Building, Feldspar
Close, Enderby, Leicestershire, LE19 4SD
Tel: 0116 275 4000
www.dmccreative.co.uk
*For DMC fabrics, bands, stranded cotton
(floss) and Light Effects threads*

Fred Aldous Ltd
37 Lever Street, Manchester, M1 1LW
Tel: 0161 236 4224
www.fredaldous.co.uk
For felt

Impressive Crafts Ltd
Unit 1 James Watt Close, Gapton Hall
Industrial Estate, Great Yarmouth,
Norfolk, NR31 0NX
Tel: 01493 441166
www.impressivecrafts.com
For aperture cards

MacCulloch & Wallis
25–26 Dering Street, London, W1S 1AT
Tel: 020 7629 0311
www.macculloch-wallis.co.uk
For haberdashery

Willow Fabrics
95 Town Lane, Mobberley, Knutsford,
Cheshire, WA16 7HH
Tel UK: 0800 0567811
Tel international: +44 (0)1565 87 22 25
www.willowfabrics.com
*For fabrics, bands, threads and
Mill Hill beads*

USA

Charles Craft Inc
PO Box 1049, Laurenburg, NC 28353
Tel: 910 844 3521
Email: ccraft@carolina.net
www.charlescraft.com
*For fabrics for cross stitch and many
useful pre-finished items (Coats Crafts
UK supply some Charles Craft products
in the UK)*

The DMC Corporation
77 South Hackensack Avenue, Bldg. 10F,
South Kearny, NJ 07032-4688
Tel: 973-589-0606
www.dmc-usa.com
For DMC fabrics, bands and threads

Jesse James and Co Inc
Email: jessejamesbutton@rcn.com
www.jessejamesbutton.com
*For 'Dress It Up' novelty buttons, also
available in some craft, scrapbooking
and quilting shops*

**Mill Hill, a division of Wichelt
Imports Inc**
N162 Hwy 35, Stoddard WI 54658
Tel: 608 788 4600
Email: millhill@millhill.com
www.millhill.com
*For Mill Hill beads and a US source for
Framecraft products*

Acknowledgments

I would like to thank DMC Creative World Ltd for their generosity in supplying all fabrics and threads used for the projects in this book. At David & Charles, my thanks go to my commissioning editor, Cheryl Brown, and to Lin Clements, my project editor, for editing the book and preparing the charts.

About the Author

Claire studied knitwear design at college before joining the design team at DMC, and finally going freelance. Claire's work has appeared in several magazines, including *Cross Stitch Magic*. Her designs also feature in six David & Charles books: *Cross Stitch Greetings Cards*, *Cross Stitch Alphabets*, *Cross Stitch Angels*, *Cross Stitch Fairies*, *Magical Cross Stitch* and *Quick to Stitch Cross Stitch Cards*, and in her solo books *Cross Stitch Card Collection*, *Picture Your Pet in Cross Stitch* and *Christmas Cross Stitch*, also published by David & Charles. Claire lives in Gunnislake, Cornwall.

Index